ROGER ELLSWORTH

People in the
Passion
of Jesus

DayOne

© Day One Publications 2007

First printed 2007

ISBN 978-1-84625-061-3

9 781846 250613 >

British Library Cataloguing in Publication Data available

Published by Day One Publications
Ryelands Road, Leominster, HR6 8NZ
Telephone 01568 613 740   FAX 01568 611 473

email—sales@dayone.co.uk
web site—www.dayone.co.uk

Cover designed by Kathryn Chedgzoy
Designed by Steve Devane and printed by Gutenberg Press, Malta.

Appreciations

In an inspiring way, Roger Ellsworth shares his clear and practical insights into the events surrounding the passion of Jesus Christ. Christians will find it informative and inspiring, and a most useful resource for sharing with family and friends the good news of the death and resurrection of Jesus Christ. I believe God will use it to bring many to salvation through faith in his Son—I highly recommend that everyone read it, share it, and discuss it at every opportunity!

Lanny Faulkner, Director of Missions, Central Baptist Association, Decatur, Illinois

This is my kind of book because it has been born in the context of prayer in the study and preaching in the church.

It is absolutely clear what its purpose is—to draw us all into the intimacy and meaning of the Lord Jesus Christ's death on the cross by observing the reactions of a range of people who were caught up in this momentous event.

I pray that the Lord will use the teaching of this book to bring peace to those who have picked it up out of general interest and spiritual enrichment to those who have been following the way of the cross for very many years.

Michael Bentley, Bracknell, England, retired minister and author of several books

Acknowledgements

The following chapters were originally presented as sermons to the Immanuel Baptist Church. I am grateful to the Lord for the enthusiasm these dear saints have for the preaching of God's Word.

As always, I am indebted to my wife Sylvia for her warm encouragement and her kind assistance.

My sincere thanks also go to Day One Publications for allowing me to participate in their vital work. May God continue to bless their efforts!

Both profoundly simple and simply profound, this is a much needed, must-read book and a perfect gift for family and friends. I highly recommend it for ministers, bible teachers, and anyone who is seriously considering the truth claims of Jesus Christ. If you only have time to read one book this year about the life and death of Jesus Christ, this ought to be it!

Contents

Dedication

To my granddaughter,
Emmalee Ruth Ellsworth.
May God bless you, dear one, with
a lifelong passion for the Passion.

Introduction

We can be glad for Mel Gibson's film, *The Passion of the Christ*, in at least one respect: it has familiarized many with the term 'Passion'. They now know it refers to the suffering of Jesus Christ. How did his suffering come to be called the 'Passion'? The answer is that our word 'passion' comes from the Latin word 'passio', which means 'suffering'.

The Passion of Christ is an inexhaustible subject. Preachers have preached, authors have written, scholars have studied—and all their efforts amount to a mere scratching of the surface.

I am asking you to join me in looking at the Passion through the lens of the people most closely associated with it.

I am inviting two groups to join me on this little journey: If you are not a believer in Christ, I ask you to come along. I want to bring you to Christ. I want to say: 'Look at what Jesus did for sinners. Does this not win your heart?'

If you are a believer in Christ, I want to be used of God to spur you onward in your Christian life. In pointing you to the Passion, I want to say: 'Look at this! Such a Saviour! Such a cost! Do you not want to do better in serving him?'

As we look at people associated with the Passion, it is my prayer that God himself will help us to be more passionate about the Passion.

1. Satan

Matthew 16:21–23

If you were asked to make a list of those most closely associated with the Passion of Christ, would you have thought to include Satan? He was definitely involved! From God's first announcement of the Passion, Satan has been intensely interested in thwarting it.

The Lord God himself first announced the Passion to Adam and Eve after they fell into sin. He announced that the seed of the woman, the Lord Jesus (Galatians 4:4), would crush the serpent's head (Genesis 3:15).

We cannot go into detail about how much Satan knew about the cross and how much he did not know. We do not have the line to fathom that depth. Suffice it to say, he knew enough about it to realize that he had to stop it at all costs. He knew that the Son of God coming into human history as the seed of the woman would constitute the deathblow to him and his kingdom.

The Old Testament is the account of God moving towards the fulfilment of his promise to send his Son. It is simultaneously the account of Satan feverishly working to thwart the promise. It is the account of the dragon seeking to devour the child (Revelation 12:1–6).

It frequently looked as if Satan would succeed. God determined that Israel would be the nation through which his

Son would come. So Satan focused on destroying that nation. Her years of bondage in Egypt and, centuries later, her seventy years of captivity in Babylon, are two such attempts.

God also determined that his Son would be a descendant of King David. So Satan also sought to destroy that line. It appeared from time to time that he would succeed. Queen Athaliah's attempt to destroy the Davidic line (2 Kings 11; 2 Chronicles 22–23) and the Babylonian captivity constituted major threats, but the line of David survived both, and the Lord Jesus arrived on the stage of human history in 'the fullness of the time' (Galatians 4:4). Jesus came, and he wasn't even late!

With the Lord Jesus on the scene, Satan focused his attention on diverting him from the cross. That strategy is apparent in the verses of our text.

JESUS STEPS TO THE PULPIT (V. 21)[1]

THE CONTENT OF HIS PROCLAMATION
The pulpit is the place of proclamation, and here we have Jesus proclaiming his death.

His words give evidence of very complete and thorough knowledge. His death would be in Jerusalem, and it would be at the hands of the religious leaders. It would also feature many sufferings.

His words also give evidence of his sense of appointment. He 'must go' to Jerusalem. Some mistakenly think that Jesus came to this earth with the intention of offering himself to his people as their earthly king. Supposedly surprised by their rejection of him, Jesus had to 'fall back' on the cross. In this scheme, the cross was 'Plan B'.

This is all wrong. The Bible tells us that Jesus was 'the Lamb slain from the foundation of the world' (Revelation 13:8).

The cross was in the mind and heart of God before the world began, and Jesus came to this earth with his eye fixed on that cross and for the express purpose of going there. His Father had made an appointment with him and that cross, and Jesus would not allow anything to keep him from that appointment.

THE PLACE OF HIS PROCLAMATION

It is interesting that Jesus spoke about his impending death at Caesarea Philippi. Its very name tells us that it was a centre for worship of the Roman Caesar. It was also a centre of worship for the Syrian Baal and the Greek god 'Pan'.

This, then, was the place of religious pluralism. It was the perfect place for Jesus to say something along these lines: 'You see, there are many religions, and each has its own special and distinct contribution to make, and each is valid. We must be glad for this pluralism and let it enrich our lives.'

It is quite significant that Jesus deliberately chose the place of religious diversity to proclaim a narrow message. He claimed to be the Messiah (vv. 16–17) who had come to die on the cross (v. 21). He further claimed that he was the one whom others should follow (v. 24), and that their refusal to do so would result in them losing their souls (v. 26).

SATAN STEPS TO THE PULPIT (V. 22)

No sooner had Jesus delivered the message about his forthcoming death on the cross than Satan stepped up to object. He did so by using Simon Peter to say: 'Far be it from You, Lord; this shall not happen to You' (v. 22).

PEOPLE IN THE PASSION OF JESUS

This is a sad thing. Simon Peter is just moments away from having brilliantly confessed the truth about Jesus: 'You are the Christ, the Son of the living God' (v. 16).

Let us learn from this how very weak and feeble the saints of God are, and how very quickly they can stumble and tumble!

What a remarkable sight we have here! Jesus speaks about the cross, and Simon takes him by the arm, steers him aside—as a parent might a child!—and tells him, Jesus, that he is mistaken! If he would listen to himself for a split second, he would realize his folly: 'Far be it from you, Lord ...' In one breath, he both calls Jesus 'Lord' and tells him he is wrong! It always sounds strange when a servant says: 'No, Lord.'

Part of Jesus' messiahship was the role of prophet, that is, one who declares the truth of God. Simon Peter has just declared him to be the Messiah, but when he, Jesus, functions as the Messiah, Simon objects. He talks and acts as if he knows more than the Christ! The scene drips with irony.

What was Satan's purpose in using Simon? It was, as we have already noted, to divert Jesus from the cross. Satan clearly regarded a crucified Christ as the ultimate disaster for his kingdom. Now if Satan regards the crucified Christ in such a way, should we not regard that same Christ in exactly the opposite way? If the crucified Christ was Satan's nightmare, should he not be our glory? How many of us are actually glorying in this Christ?

JESUS DRIVES SATAN FROM THE PULPIT (V. 23)

How does Jesus respond to Simon's rebuke? Does he congratulate him on his insight and thank him for his contribution? Not at all! He rebukes him in no uncertain terms: 'Get behind me, Satan! You are an offence to Me, for you are not mindful of the things of God, but the things of men.'

So Jesus identified both the cross as 'the things of God', and all those who oppose it as 'Satan'.

And he reminded Simon Peter that the proper place for the disciple is always behind his master. The disciple is to follow, not lead! Satan had got behind Simon and pushed him out in front of Jesus to lead, and Jesus is now pushing Simon back to his rightful place.

By the way, there is tremendous comfort in the Lord Jesus exposing Satan by rebuking Simon. This shows us that the preaching of the cross will not perish from the earth. No matter how Satan attacks, he will never be able to destroy the saving message of the cross.

Centuries have come and gone since that ancient day in Caesarea Philippi, but little has changed. The Lord Jesus is still sending his message out into this world. It is still the message of his cross. He declares that no one can stand acceptably in the presence of the holy God unless his sins are forgiven, and that the only way for sins to be forgiven is through that cross. The Lord Jesus tells us that he died there in the place of sinners. He took their penalty, the penalty of separation from God, so those sinners who will come to him in repentance and faith will not have to endure that penalty themselves.

Satan is also sending out his message. It is the message that scorns and ridicules that cross. Every time a minister stands in a pulpit to minimize the cross or in any way to deny it, Satan's leering face can be seen behind him.

The two messages still go out, and the choice still remains.

Will we listen to the message of the cross or the message that despises it? And let those who dare stand in pulpits answer this question: Will we preach the crucified Christ, or will we preach as if we know more than the one we call 'Lord'?

Note

1 I am indebted to Klaas Schilder for the idea of the pulpit: **Klaas Schilder,** *Christ in His Suffering* (Grand Rapids: Eerdmans, 1938), pp. 15–22.

2. Caiaphas

John 11:47–52

Things were at fever pitch in Jerusalem. Jesus had raised the dead Lazarus in the nearby village of Bethany. The religious leaders of Jerusalem knew something had to be done about Jesus, and done quickly! The meeting of one of these men, Caiaphas, with Jesus is fascinating for several reasons, one of which is the unique glimpse that it gives us of another meeting—that of heaven and hell!

There is no wider gap in all of reality than the gap between heaven and hell.

- Heaven is the place of God and the angels; hell, the place of the devil and his demons.
- Heaven is the place of holiness; hell, the place of sin.
- Heaven is the place of the saints; hell, the place of sinners.
- Heaven is the place of light; hell, the place of darkness.
- Heaven is the place of no suffering; hell, the place of incredible suffering.
- Heaven is the place of happiness; hell, the place of sorrow.
- Heaven is high; hell is so low that it is sometimes described as 'the bottomless pit'.

The history of the human race is one long record of disagreement between heaven and hell.

- Heaven says God is good; hell says he is not.

- Heaven says the Word of God is true; hell denies it.
- Heaven says the earth was created by God; hell says it is the product of chance.
- Heaven affirms that man is God's special creation, made in the image of God; hell says he is merely the highest of the animals.
- Heaven declares that sin is serious; hell laughs it off.
- Heaven proclaims that Jesus is God in human flesh; hell declares him to be mere man.
- Heaven says heaven and hell are real places; hell affirms them to be figments of the imaginations of deluded people.

With such a vast distance between heaven and hell, we should not expect to ever find any agreement between them at all. But the passage with which we are dealing brings before us an amazing thing. Heaven and hell do come together in agreement. Klass Schilder puts it like this: 'A cry rises from the depths of hell; a cry sounds from the heights of heaven. It is the same cry ...'[1]

What is this cry? It is the cry that Jesus must die. Schilder says: 'At both tribunals, that above and that below, the verdict reads alike.'[2]

THE MESSAGE OF HELL

Caiaphas, the high priest of Israel, is the spokesman for hell in this passage.

Caiaphas was a man with a very large problem. The raising of Lazarus from the dead constituted powerful proof that Jesus was indeed the Messiah. The religious leaders were now faced with the possibility of many turning to Jesus (v. 48). Why did this concern them? If Jesus were too widely regarded as the

Messiah who was out to set up his own kingdom, the Romans would come in and crush Israel and remove those who were in power, namely, Caiaphas and his cohorts (v. 48).

So Caiaphas carefully weighed the situation and came up with this conclusion: Jesus had to die. To his way of thinking, it came down to destroying one man to keep the whole nation from being destroyed.

Caiaphas was calling for substitution! Jesus was to die so others would not have to die!

And when those words tumbled from his lips, all of heaven exploded in applause. For the first time in its history, hell was finally right!

Yes, but it goes beyond that. Those words came from heaven! God broke in and took over Caiaphas' mouth so that he declared God's truth (v. 51).

THE MESSAGE OF HEAVEN

Heaven also called for the death of Jesus. When did heaven begin this call? From before the foundation of the world (Acts 2:22–23; Revelation 13:8)!

But why would heaven call for the death of Jesus? Human sin! God cannot ignore sin. His holy character will not allow him to do so. The penalty for sin must be paid, and the penalty is nothing less than eternal separation from God. It is God's wrath for ever.

That penalty has to be paid before the sinner can ever enter into fellowship with God. Either the sinner must pay it himself, or someone must pay it on his behalf.

In grace that is far beyond our ability to comprehend, God sent Jesus to receive that penalty on behalf of sinners. In other words, Jesus came to be the substitute for sinners. On the cross he received an eternity's worth of wrath for all who abandon their sins and trust in him alone as their Saviour.

Jesus was on the cross from nine in the morning until three in the afternoon. How could he in the space of six hours receive an eternity's amount of wrath for all believers? We can never begin to fathom this. All we can say is that the Lord Jesus was unique. He was God in human flesh. As God, he was an infinite person, and as an infinite person, he could suffer in a finite amount of time an infinite amount of wrath.

While we cannot understand this, we can and must believe it. On the day that Caiaphas spoke, both hell and heaven agreed. Jesus must die for others. Yes, the motives of hell and heaven were different, but their messages were the same.

The question now is: do we agree? To put it another way, are we willing to join the united voices of hell and heaven? Are we willing to say that Jesus had to die for others, and that our only hope for forgiveness of sins and entrance into heaven is that he died in our stead? Are we willing to take as our own these words:

> O Christ, what burdens bowed thy head!
> our load was laid on thee;
> Thou stoodest in the sinner's stead,
> didst bear all ill for me.
> A victim led, thy blood was shed!
> Now there's no load for me.
>
> Death and the curse were in our cup:
> O Christ, 'twas full for thee!

But thou hast drained the last dark drop,
'tis empty now for me:
That bitter cup, love drank it up,
now blessing's draught for me.

Jehovah lifted up his rod:
O Christ, it fell on thee!
Thou wast sore stricken of thy God;
There's not one stroke for me.
Thy tears, thy blood beneath it flowed;
Thy bruising healeth me.

(Anne Ross Cousin).

Are we willing to say with Philip Bliss:

Bearing shame and scoffing rude
in my place condemned he stood;
sealed my pardon with his blood:
Hallelujah! what a Saviour!

Notes

1 **Klaas Schilder,** *Christ in His Suffering*, p. 61.
2 Ibid.

3. Mary of Bethany

John 12:1–8

The anointing of Jesus by Mary occurred in Bethany at the house of Simon the leper (Matthew 26:6). Having been healed, we presume, by Jesus, Simon chose this way to honour him. He also invited Mary, Martha, and Lazarus. Since Jesus had raised Lazarus from the dead a few days earlier, Lazarus and his sisters would have welcomed the opportunity to share in honouring Jesus. In fact, it appears that Lazarus also was an honoured guest (v. 2).

Martha, of course, was busy serving (v. 2), but apparently without the anxiety and distraction of a former time (Luke 10:38).

And Mary was again at Jesus' feet. G. Campbell Morgan says: 'She sat at his feet, when the sun was shining. Then when the darkness was round about her, and Lazarus was dead, and her heart was breaking, she came when he sent for her, and went straight to his feet. Now it was his day of approaching sorrow, and again she went straight to his feet.'[1]

This time, however, Mary was at his feet not only to listen, but also to give concrete expression to her love for him. She took a pound of very expensive ointment and anointed his head (Matthew 26:7) and his feet. She then loosed the long tresses of her hair and proceeded to use them to dry the feet of

Jesus. Judas and some of the others (Matthew 26:8) protested vigorously against this 'waste', but Jesus defended it.

Such a lavish, uninhibited expression of love deserves closer scrutiny, for the truth is that very few of us love Christ as we should, and it's urgent that we begin to do so. Therefore, let's try to go back through time and put ourselves there with Jesus, Mary and the others. Let's notice first:

WHAT PROMPTED THIS EXPRESSION OF LOVE

Two strong factors combined in Mary's heart and drove her to this expression of love.

GRATITUDE

The more obvious of the two was her gratitude for what Jesus had done for her and her family. Mary had so much for which to thank Jesus. He had visited their home on more than one occasion. He had instructed them in the things of God. When Lazarus died Jesus spoke words of comfort and hope (John 11:25–26) and proceeded to raise him from the dead. All of these things and more must have gone racing through her mind as she sat there watching Jesus and Lazarus, listening to them talk and laugh. Overwhelmed with the realization of what she owed Jesus, Mary slipped away, took the prized ointment, and returned to anoint Jesus.

UNDERSTANDING

Mary's act was also prompted by understanding. She had procured this ointment especially for the time of Jesus' burial. That's the only logical explanation for Jesus' words: 'She has kept this for the day of My burial' (v. 7).

PEOPLE IN THE PASSION OF JESUS

On this night she evidently realized his death was near. Morgan suggests that she looked into his eyes and 'saw the sorrow there'.[2]

She must also have realized that there was a strong possibility that his enemies would not allow his body to be anointed. She concluded, then, that there would never be another opportunity better than the one at that time.

Jesus had often predicted his death at the hand of his enemies (Matthew 16:21; Mark 8:31–32; 9:12; 10:32–34; John 6:52–56; 7:33; 8:21–23), but only Mary seemed to really understand, prompting William Hendriksen to remark: 'Mary was, perhaps, the best listener Jesus ever had.'[3]

If Mary felt such gratitude, shouldn't we? Has Christ done any less for those of us who are saved than he did for her? No, we have not had any family members raised from the dead, but all who know Christ have had their dead souls quickened (Ephesians 2:1–7); and in due time we shall have all our brothers and sisters in Christ raised from the dead (1 Thessalonians 4:13–18)!

If Mary had such an understanding of Christ, shouldn't we? She came to her understanding without the benefit of a complete disclosure of the necessity and meaning of Jesus' death. We, on the other hand, have in the Bible everything we need to know about Jesus' death. We can read about the cross being the very wisdom and power of God (1 Corinthians 1:18–25). What Mary saw faintly, we can see clearly.

If we feel gratitude to Jesus as Mary did, and if we understand Jesus even better than she did, why do we not show the same sacrificial, self-forgetful love she did? That is the burning question! The main issue before our churches today is whether we have a passionate love for Christ.

PEOPLE IN THE PASSION OF JESUS

So Mary's expression of love was prompted by gratitude and understanding. But let's turn now to consider:

WHAT THIS EXPRESSION OF LOVE PROMPTED

It didn't take long for Mary's action to create a reaction! Acts of love for Christ seldom go undetected or unchallenged. Mary's action set off a wave of criticism. Judas professed to be indignant over such unscrupulous waste. He took this opportunity to portray himself as a champion of the downtrodden (vv. 4–5). John tells us that Judas was not as great a champion of the poor as he pretended to be: 'This he said, not that he cared for the poor, but because he was a thief, and had the money box; and he used to take what was put in it' (v. 6). At that time, however, the other disciples were unaware of what a sinister rascal he was, and they were persuaded by his 'humanitarian' appeal (Matthew 26:8; Mark 14:4–5). So Mary had to contend with not one, but several critics. The apostle Paul says love 'bears all things' and 'endures all things' (1 Corinthians 13:7). Mary's love certainly had a lot to bear and endure!

But over against the sting of criticism came a soothing commendation from the Lord himself. How often he grieved over the ignorance, faithlessness and lovelessness of his disciples. But here was a disciple who really understood and who loved without limits. When the critics spoke up, Jesus immediately came to her defence. All who love the Lord as fully as Mary may rest assured that he delights in defending them also from satanic attack.

Surely the Lord must be grieved today that so few of us express our love without reservation. I fear many of us are

Laodicean Christians. We have become lukewarm in our affection to Christ (Revelation 3:14–22). How refreshing it would be to our Lord if he could see a rekindling of our first love.

Mary's act also had to have a profound impact on the disciples. First, it taught them the urgency of love. It forced them to evaluate their priorities. Jesus said: 'For the poor you have with you always; but Me you do not have always' (v. 8).

Can you imagine how those words, 'me you do not have always', must have returned time after time to awaken these disciples with a start, to haunt their minds and to stab their consciences? But these poignant words didn't have an immediate effect on the disciples, for a few nights later they slept while Jesus prayed in agony. We are so slow to learn the lesson Mary teaches—to love while we can.

Thomas Carlyle had neglected his wife over the years. One day she was suddenly snatched from him. Only then did Carlyle realize what he had so long taken for granted. Hear the solemn words of Carlyle: 'Cherish what is dearest while you have it near you, and wait not till it is far away. Blind and deaf that we are, O think, if thou yet love anybody living, wait not till death sweep down the paltry little dust clouds and dissonances of the moment, and all be made at last so mournfully clear and beautiful, when it is too late.'4

Jesus wasn't calling his disciples to neglect the poor, but rather to a sensitivity of the preciousness of that moment. He was urging them not to let the good, the feeding of the poor, become the enemy of the best, loving and worshiping him. They were in danger of subjecting the unique and urgent to the usual and constant. Matthew Henry writes: 'That good duty which may be done at any time ought to give way to that which cannot be done but just now.'[5]

Such is the urgency of love. But Mary's act also taught the disciples the fervency of love. Mary allowed her heart to speak freely in this act. We are so prone to temper our love, to be half-hearted in it. The major hindrance to the cause of Christ in our day is the half-hearted love of his disciples. If we would learn from Mary to love fervently without hesitation or reservation, the kingdom of our Lord would advance with mind-boggling success!

The more I think about Mary and her love for Christ, the more I agree with Morgan: 'I would rather be in succession to Mary of Bethany than to the whole crowd of the apostles.'[6]

Notes

1 **G. Campbell Morgan,** *The Gospel According to John* (New York: Fleming H. Revell, 1933), p. 207.

2 Ibid. p. 208.

3 **William Hendriksen,** *New Testament Commentary: John* (Grand Rapids: Baker Book House, 1954), p. 180.

4 Cited by **Clarence Edward Macartney,** 'Come before Winter', in *20 Centuries of Great Preaching,* ed. Clyde E. Fant, Jr (Waco: Word Books, 1971), vol. ix, p. 137.

5 **Matthew Henry,** *Matthew Henry's Commentary* (Fleming H. Revell Company), vol. v, p. 1070.

6 **Morgan,** *John,* p. 208.

4. Judas Iscariot[1]

Mark 14:10–11, 43–46

Judas Iscariot is one of the most tragic figures in all of human history. Having been chosen as one of Jesus' original twelve disciples, and having followed him for three-and-a-half-years, Judas betrayed him for thirty pieces of silver. But his story does not end there. A few hours after his despicable act, Judas came back to the religious leaders who paid him, dashed the thirty coins to the ground, and went out and hanged himself.

The thirty pieces of silver were used to purchase a field in which Judas was buried. This was all Judas had to show for his treason—a place to be buried! Something he would have had even if he had not betrayed the Lord!

I recently heard about a man who preached his own funeral. There he was lying in the casket, and, when the time for the service came, one of his sons walked up to the pulpit and pushed the 'Play' button on a tape recorder. And the people heard the voice of the dear departed! This was a fulfilment of the verse that says 'he, being dead, yet speaketh'!

Judas has been dead for more than 2,000 years. And yet there is a sense in which he is still speaking! What does Judas have to say? What lessons can we learn from the dead Judas?

WE CAN HAVE GREAT SPIRITUAL PRIVILEGES, YET BE FOREVER LOST

What spiritual privileges he enjoyed! One of those privileges lay in hearing what he heard—the greatest truths from the greatest of all preachers! Judas Iscariot heard those teachings that astonished so many. He heard the matchless Sermon on the Mount and its chilling warning about being deceived (Matthew 7:21–23). He heard Jesus plainly tell his hearers of judgement to come, and the need to repent and place their trust in him (e.g. Luke 13:1–5), but while others trembled and repented, Judas did not.

When a multitude became offended at the teaching of Jesus and ceased following him, Simon Peter stayed with him because he heard in those same teachings the authentic ring of eternal life (John 6:68). Judas Iscariot heard those same words, and, while he also stayed with Jesus, it was not because of those words.

Another of those privileges lay in seeing what he saw. The sick healed! The multitudes fed! Storms stilled! The dead raised! Perhaps the most touching of all was on the night before Jesus was crucified, when Judas saw Jesus kneel before him and tenderly wash his feet (John 13:1–5). That wondrous act of condescension and service was followed by Jesus plainly declaring to Judas, that he, Jesus, was fully aware of what he was about to do (John 13:26–27).

But nothing stopped Judas. He left the room immediately after Jesus spoke to him, and the apostle John, recording the event years later, put this wrap on Judas' departure: 'And it was night' (John 13:30). Indeed it was. The darkness of the night was no match for the darkness of Judas' soul. With it all, Judas was still an unsaved man (John 6:70–71).

PEOPLE IN THE PASSION OF JESUS

We can think of Judas in yet another way. We can say that he went a long way in religion only to be finally lost. Hebrews 6:4–6 warns about this possibility. We can all go a long way in religion and be lost! Think about Judas as an example of the truth of these verses:

- He was enlightened. He heard the truth from Jesus.
- He tasted of the heavenly gift, actually witnessing the power of heaven at work.
- He partook of the Holy Spirit. The Lord Jesus was endued with the Spirit of God (John 3:34), and to the extent that Judas received and appreciated the ministry of Jesus, he partook of that gift.
- He tasted the good word of God. He heard the Word of God from Jesus, and to some extent actually enjoyed it.
- He tasted the power of the age to come. The signs and wonders performed by Jesus clearly pointed him beyond this earthly realm to the heavenly realm.

Judas was an extremely blessed man. He had remarkable spiritual privileges, but he never truly came to faith in the redeeming work that Jesus had come to do. After leading the authorities to Jesus, he admitted that he had betrayed 'innocent blood' (Matthew 27:4), but he never took refuge in that blood.

WE MUST ACCEPT THE LORD JESUS AS HE IS, NOT AS WE WANT HIM TO BE

Why did Judas betray Jesus? Why, after hearing all he heard and seeing all he saw, did he turn against Jesus? He obviously was not interested in the kind of kingdom Jesus was offering.

Judas was interested in material things, and he wanted Jesus to set up a material, temporal kingdom. When he saw Jesus setting up a spiritual kingdom, a kingdom in which he graciously received sinners, Judas became more and more disappointed and disillusioned.

Some think that Judas' betrayal of Jesus was designed to put Jesus into a corner with the authorities so that he, Jesus, would have to use his power to set up the kind of kingdom Judas wanted.

Whatever course we follow in seeking to explain Judas' action, we must not lose sight of the main thing. S.G. DeGraaf puts it powerfully: 'Judas was an unbeliever! Enthusiastically he had followed Christ as a disciple ... Yet, he had closed his heart to what was essential in Christ, to the grace of God in him, and therefore he had not been able or willing to believe in him.'[2]

Some take exception to this. They insist that Judas was a genuine believer in Christ, that his act of betrayal should not be considered to be any worse than Simon Peter's denial of Christ. In other words, they contend that Judas was a believer who sinned rather than an unbeliever. The Bible, however, gives us no room to wriggle on this matter. The Lord Jesus himself referred to Judas as a 'devil' (John 6:70) and 'the son of perdition' (John 17:12). These are not terms that can be applied to the saints of God, even when they falter and fail as Simon Peter did.

It is interesting to draw parallels between Judas and Ahithophel who rebelled against King David.[3] When Ahithophel realized that David would return to the throne of Israel—even though David was unworthy and sinful!—Ahithophel ended his life. He did so out of angry bitterness against the grace of God that would restore a wretch like David.

Judas saw that same grace in the ministry of Jesus, and, like Ahithophel, could not stand it. As we think about these two men, Ahithophel and Judas, we must ask ourselves if we can accept the gospel of grace that says man can never save himself!

Because Judas was content with only an outward show of allegiance to Christ and was not a genuine believer in him and his redemption, he came to a terrible end. Scripture tells us that he went out and hanged himself (Matthew 27:1–10), but that was not his end.

Terrible and gruesome as that act was, it could not compare with the hell that yawned to receive his soul. That same fate awaits all those who join Judas in his rejection of Christ (2 Thessalonians 1:8–10). Let us, therefore, beware of doing as Judas did—putting too little value on Jesus.

Notes

1 This chapter is similar to my chapter on Judas Iscariot in *How to Live in a Dangerous World* (Darlington: Evangelical Press, 1998), pp. 94–99.

2 **S. G. DeGraaf,** *Promise and Deliverance* (Presbyterian and Reformed Publishing Co.), vol. iii, pp. 152–53.

3 I am indebted to Klass Schilder for this comparison. Please see **Klaas Schilder,** *Christ on Trial* (Grand Rapids: Eerdmans, 1939), pp. 249–256.

5. Simon Peter[1]

John 18:15–18,25–27

It is certainly one of the saddest episodes in the Bible. Given the opportunity to stand up and speak up for Christ, Simon Peter failed. Not once did he fail, not twice, but three times.

There was so much Simon could have said about the Lord Jesus Christ. He was there when Jesus turned water into wine (John 2:1–11). He was there when Jesus healed his mother-in-law of a high fever (Luke 4:38–39).

Simon Peter had seen Jesus feed five thousand with five barley loaves and two small fish (John 6:1–13). He was there when Jesus walked on the stormy sea (John 6:15–21). He was there on the Mount of Transfiguration when Jesus glistened with heavenly glory (Luke 9:28–35).

Peter had seen Jesus heal the lame (John 5:1–9) and the blind (John 9:1–7). He had even seen Jesus raise three people from the dead (Mark 5:39–42; Luke 7:11–15; John 11:43–44), one of whom had been dead four days (John 11:39).

In addition to all these things, Simon Peter had, by his own admission, heard in the words of Jesus the authentic ring of the message of eternal life (John 6:68).

Simon Peter could have talked about all these things and many, many more. He could have responded to the inquiry of the servant girl and those with her by affirming that he, Simon

Peter, was a disciple of Jesus Christ and that he was glad to be in that number. He could have said that knowing Jesus was the supreme treasure of his life, that no matter how many days he had remaining, he knew of a certainty that nothing else would approach the inestimable privilege that he had in those days in which he walked with the Lord Jesus.

THE SHAMEFUL DENIALS

Yes, that is what he could have said, but he did not. He had the opportunity to stand firm for Christ and bear witness, but he faltered and failed. He had the opportunity to be a solid rock, but, in the words of Kent Hughes, he proved to be 'a cracked rock'.[2]

How shameful were Peter's three denials! He did not even attempt to soften them. He could have said, 'You have me confused with someone else' or 'I don't know what you are talking about.' But he spat his denials out in the most unambiguous and emphatic way imaginable: 'I am not!' (vv. 17, 25). Matthew tells us that Peter went so far as to lace his denials with cursing (Matthew 26:74).

THE REASON FOR THE DENIALS

Why did Simon Peter do it? Why did he deny the very one to whom he owed so much? Why did he refuse to confess his allegiance to the one who had rescued him from sin and so often thrilled him with joy unspeakable and full of glory? Biblical commentators have ranged over a good bit of ground in seeking to explain the reason for Simon's denials. Some point out that he had been very proud and self-confident that very night (Mark 14:29–31), and that pride always precedes a fall. Some suggest that it was all due to the fact that he had been sleeping when he should have been praying (Mark 14:37–38). Some observe that he had set himself up for failure by warming himself at the fire of those who obviously were not friends of Jesus (Mark 14:67; Luke 22:55). Some affirm that all of these considerations must be factored in to any explanation for Peter's denials.

PETER'S FEAR

While we may see some legitimacy in all of these, they do seem to miss the most obvious thing, that is, Peter's fear. He was afraid of what might happen to him if he professed allegiance to Jesus. By this time Jesus' predictions of his death (Matthew 16:21; 17:22–23; 20:17–19) must have finally flooded in upon Peter. He now knew of a certainty that Jesus was going to die, and he was afraid that, if he admitted to being his disciple, he would die right along with him. The looming spectre of dying alongside Jesus drove Peter right away from confessing Jesus.

OUR FEARS AND DENIALS

All of this hits painfully close to home. Every Christian knows what it is to be afraid of what will happen if we let our allegiance to Christ be known—afraid of what others will think or say about us, afraid that we will be thought to be unsophisticated, narrow, biased and benighted, afraid that we might be deprived of that job over there or that promotion, afraid that we will be considered to be out of step. So it is very easy to pretend either that we have no allegiance to Christ at all or that we have not allowed what allegiance we have to take us to extremes.

PEOPLE IN THE PASSION OF JESUS

There are many ways of hiding or misrepresenting that allegiance. It can be something as simple as not wanting someone to see that we have a Bible in our possession. It can be a matter of using profanity, and by so doing essentially saying: 'I don't want anyone to know that I belong to Christ, so I will talk as if I don't.' It can be a matter of maintaining silence when our Lord is attacked and vilified, that is, acting as if we approve of what is being said.

Every Lord's Day the children of God are faced with this blunt question: Will I this day let my allegiance to Christ be known by going to public worship? Or, to put it another way, every Lord's Day we are confronted with this question: Am I going to let other interests and allegiances (such as athletic events and family activities) take priority over my allegiance to Christ and his church?

Sometimes the temptation to deny Christ comes in the form of denying his teachings. For instance, we are commanded to forgive those who trespass against us (Matthew 6:12; 18:21–22). If we refuse to do so, we deny our Lord.

In this area of our Lord's teachings, we must also note that we deny him when we feel compelled to remove or downplay those truths that we consider to be offensive to those around us. We may, for example, find it very attractive to say to those around us: 'Yes, I am a Christian, but I don't believe in all that stuff about judgement and hell.'

These and similar situations are not easy for us, but we can stand for Christ in them. We do not have to fail as Peter did. Queen Esther in the Old Testament faced a situation much like the one in which Simon Peter found himself, but she did not fail:

AN EXAMPLE OF BOLDNESS

Because of his bitterness against the Jew Mordecai, Haman, the prime minister of Persia, hoodwinked the king into issuing a decree that all the Jews be executed (Esther 3:1–15). Little did he know that Esther herself was a Jew (Esther 2:20).

This situation demanded that Esther go before the king and intercede for her people, but there was a large problem. Anyone who came into the king's presence without being summoned by him would be put to death unless the king extended his sceptre (Esther 4:11), and Esther had not been summoned for a period of thirty days. But Esther, believing she had been brought to the kingdom for that very hour (Esther 4:14), summoned courage and went to the king on behalf of her people. Confronted with the opportunity to deny her connection with her people, she boldly confessed it. How refreshingly different from Simon Peter!

THE BITTER CONSEQUENCES

All of us who know the Lord have denied him in one way or another, but no true Christian will ever be comfortable denying Christ. The Gospel accounts tell us that Peter's denials caused him to weep bitterly (Mark 14:72; Luke 22:62). No Christian will regard his denials of Christ as light and trivial matters. They will weigh heavily upon him and bring grief to his heart until he finds a place of repentance. Even after repentance, the memory of those denials will cause him shame. If, on the other hand, there is no sorrow over denying Christ and no repentance of it, it may indicate that we have no Christ to deny and have deceived ourselves about belonging to him.

PEOPLE IN THE PASSION OF JESUS

THE MATCHLESS GRACE OF CHRIST

We surely cannot consider Peter's denials of Christ without turning our thoughts to the final chapter of John's Gospel. Simon Peter and some of the other disciples of Jesus had gone fishing in Galilee. These men were probably at a loose end. Jesus had risen from the dead and appeared to them, but they were uncertain as to what the future held for them. Simon Peter may very well have been convinced that whatever Jesus had in mind for the other disciples, it certainly would not include him. He was in for quite a surprise.

As a long, fruitless night of fishing gave way to the dawn, he and those with him could discern a figure in the early morning mist, but they did not know it was Jesus. His command to them to cast their net on the other side of the boat and the subsequent catch was designed to remind them of his early call to them (Luke 5:1–7) and to assure them that that call had not been revoked.

Upon seeing the catch, the men realized the figure on the shore was none other than Jesus, and the impulsive Simon bailed out of the boat and made his way to him. There on the shore Simon found Jesus had built a fire (John 21:9), and there the Lord Jesus asked him, not once, not twice, but three times, whether he, Simon, loved him. It was around a fire that Peter had three times denied Christ, and now around the fire he was given the opportunity three times to confess his love for Christ (John 21:15–17).

In this way the Lord Jesus showed Simon Peter something of the greatness of his grace. It is truly grace that is greater than all our sins, and it will never, no never, let us go. It not only pursued Simon, it also restored him to usefulness and fruitfulness in the work of Christ's kingdom.

I am certainly not glad that Peter denied Christ, but since it is a fact that he did, I am glad that the Gospel writers relate it. I am glad because I can read their accounts and be reminded of the terrible power of sin in the life of the child of God and the glorious reality of the grace of God that forgives, cleanses and restores to usefulness. Even when we are faithless, he remains faithful (2 Timothy 2:13).

Notes

1 For a similar chapter, see my book *How to Live in a Dangerous World* (Darlington: Evangelical Press, 1998), pp. 211–16.

2 **R. Kent Hughes,** *Mark: Jesus, Servant and Savior* (Westchester, Ill.: Crossway Books, 1989), vol. ii, p. 183.

6. Pilate

John 18:28–19:16

As we have noted, the Jewish nation was under the control of Rome during the life and ministry of the Lord Jesus. The official policy of Rome was that the Jews could not execute criminals without Roman approval (18:31). This was one of those rules that the Jewish leadership ignored when it suited them. Acts 7 relates the Jews' execution of Stephen, and there is no indication of Rome sanctioning it.

But in the case of Jesus, the Jews were very eager to have Roman approval. The reason? Rome's method of execution was crucifixion, and to the Jews crucifixion was a sign of God's curse (Deuteronomy 21:23). As far as the religious leaders were concerned, crucifixion for Jesus would effectively end all talk of him being the Messiah. A crucified Messiah was as impossible as a square circle!

After conducting their own 'trial' and condemning Jesus to death, the religious leaders carted him off to Pilate, the Roman governor. These men were very shrewd. They knew that Pilate would have no interest in executing a man who claimed to be God. Pilate's boss, the Roman emperor, claimed the same! So they had to put the charge against Jesus in a manner that would get Pilate's attention, namely, that Jesus was claiming to be a king (Luke 23:2). This is the reason that Pilate began his interrogation of Jesus with this question: 'Are you the King of the Jews?' (18:33). Later, when Pilate tried to find a way to release Jesus, the religious leaders would become even more insistent about Jesus being a rival to Caesar (19:12).

PILATE'S INITIAL INTERROGATION (18:33–38)

With the possibility of having a rival to Caesar on his hands, Pilate wasted no time in addressing the issue, asking Jesus: 'Are you the King of the Jews?' (18:33).

Pilate wanted a 'yes' or 'no' answer, and Jesus refused to give it to him. A 'yes' would have been interpreted by Pilate in a political sense and would have made Jesus guilty as charged.

On the other hand, a 'no' would have been taken to mean that Jesus was not a king in any sense whatsoever. Jesus would not and could not deny himself. While he was not the kind of king that Pilate had in mind, he was definitely a king.

Jesus responded, therefore, by asking Pilate a question that got to the heart of the matter: 'Are you speaking for yourself about this, or did others tell you this concerning Me?' (18:34).

Jesus was asking whether Pilate was going to interpret kingship in the same way as the religious leaders, or whether he was open to another possibility.

Pilate bristled at the suggestion that the Jews could dictate to him. He was no Jew (18:35)! But he had to know the truth!

So Jesus gave him the truth. Yes, he was a king, but not in a political sense. His kingdom was not of this world. It was a spiritual kingdom (18:36). William Hendriksen explains: 'Jesus is the *real* king of the *real* Jews' (italics are his).[1] Jesus rules and reigns in the hearts of all those who truly believe in him.

Pilate's next words, 'Are You a king then?' (18:37), may

reflect his desire to know more about what Jesus was claiming. Or they may have indicated surprise and shock, as if he was saying: 'Then you really are claiming to be a king!'

Whatever Pilate's intent, his words opened the door for Jesus to elaborate: 'You say rightly that I am a king. For this cause I was born, and for this cause I have come into the world, that I should bear witness to the truth. Everyone who is of the truth hears My voice' (18:37).

Jesus affirmed that he was indeed a king, that his kingdom is built on truth, and that the citizens of his kingdom embrace that truth.

To all of that Pilate merely shrugged: 'What is truth?', and walked away (18:38).

The truth regarding the greatest of all kings—Jesus!—and the greatest of all kingdoms—the eternal kingdom of those who believe in Jesus!—hovered so tantalizingly close to Pilate, but he was not interested.

Pilate may very well have wondered about Jesus and the kingship he claimed as he walked away, but one thing he did not wonder about—Jesus was innocent of the charges that had been brought against him. He was not a rival to Caesar, and, having come back to the religious leaders, Pilate reported: 'I find no fault in him at all' (18:38).

PILATE'S ATTEMPTED COMPROMISE (18:39–19:6)

Pilate was a man with a dilemma. On one hand, he knew that Jesus had done nothing deserving of death. On the other hand, he wanted to pacify the religious leaders, who already possessed considerable hostility towards the Roman government.

Ever the shrewd politician, Pilate sought to steer a middle course between the conflicting demands. He would have his soldiers administer a flogging to Jesus before releasing him. The Jews would be happy because Jesus would be severely punished, and he, Pilate, would be happy because he would not have sentenced Jesus to die. Pilate probably thought that Jesus would also be happy to get out of the situation with his life, assuming, of course, that Jesus survived the scourging (not all did!). Little did Pilate realize that Jesus could not be happy apart from going to the cross. That cross, painful as it would be, would give joy to the Lord Jesus because it would be the means of redemption for his people.

Pilate, then, handed Jesus over to his soldiers for the scourging. These men were very good at their work, and they carried it out with grim efficiency. And then, as if to add a touch of humour to the stern business, they gave Jesus some of the trappings of royalty—a purple robe and a crown of thorns!

The battered, bleeding Jesus in his robe and crown certainly would not excite any notions of kingship. The sight of him would rather elicit only feelings of pity and effectively end any talk of kingship and the need for further punishment. At least, that is what Pilate thought when he paraded Jesus before the Jews and cried: 'Behold the Man!' (19:5).

It was Pilate's way of saying: 'Look at the poor fellow. He has suffered enough for his delusion. What need is there to proceed further?'

But Pilate's attempt to compromise fell flat on its face. The Jews could not feel pity for Jesus, only contempt, and in that contempt they cried: 'Crucify Him, crucify Him!' (19:6).

PILATE'S FINAL CAPITULATION (19:7–16)

Stunned by the ferocity of it all, Pilate repeated that he found no fault in Jesus, and if they wanted him crucified, they would have to do it themselves (19:6). But the religious leaders were not about to let Pilate off the hook. They wanted Jesus crucified, and they wanted Pilate to do it. And they would have it no other way.

Pilate made one attempt after another to release Jesus, but the insistence of the Jews that releasing Jesus was tantamount to treason to Caesar finally caused Pilate to cave in (19:12). If it was crucifixion that they wanted, it was crucifixion they would have (19:16).

Christians today find themselves in much the same position as their Lord—under attack! The attack is not so much because Christians are guilty of anything, but rather because they are hated. Unlike their Lord, they are not perfect, but, like him, they are hated. That hatred is not in itself so frightening when it is restrained by legal authority, but believers in Christ are increasingly finding that the authorities are not so much interested in the right as they are in the many, united, loud, persistent voices of hatred.

Pilate emerges from the pages of Scripture as one of its most pathetic characters. Knowing Jesus was innocent and that the religious leaders were merely looking for a way to get rid of him, Pilate still refused to stand for justice. Allowing political expediency to guide him, Pilate passed the buck by asking the multitude to decide what should happen to Jesus.

We stand in Pilate's sandals when we try to have it both ways with Jesus, knowing he is the Lord and yet refusing to submit to him.

Note

1 **William Hendriksen,** *John* (Grand Rapids: Baker Book House, 1954), p. 407.

PEOPLE IN THE PASSION OF JESUS

7. Barabbas

Luke 23:13–25

Barabbas was a dead man, and Pontius Pilate was a desperate man. I say Barabbas was a dead man because he had been sentenced to die for insurrection and murder (v. 25). Sentence had been passed, and all that lay ahead of Barabbas were a few dreary hours before it was carried out.

Pilate, on the other hand, was a desperate man. The Jewish leaders were demanding that Jesus be crucified, and Pilate knew that the man had done nothing to deserve such a fate. How to satisfy the troublesome Jews without crucifying Jesus! That was Pilate's dilemma.

Pilate was also a clever man—a shrewd politician! He would give the religious leaders a choice! He would bring both Jesus and Barabbas before the multitude and let them choose which would be released and which would be executed. It was customary at Passover time to show clemency to a prisoner (Mark 15:6).

As far as Pilate was concerned, the outcome was not in question. The crowd would ask for Jesus to be released. Jesus had gone about healing the sick, casting out demons and proclaiming the kingdom of God. Barabbas, on the other hand, was a true lowlife. The people would be glad to be rid of him.

The whole thing was perfect. Barabbas, the guilty, would receive the death he deserved, and Jesus, the innocent, would go free.

How did Barabbas spend what he considered to be his last night on earth? Did he sleep at all? Did he spend those few, fleeting hours thinking about how he had mishandled life and wondering about God, judgement and eternity? Or did he spend that time seething in rebellious anger toward God and man?

Whatever occupied him came to a screeching halt with the clanking of armour and the loud talk of Roman soldiers. They were on their way to get him, and he was on his way to a Roman cross!

BARABBAS AND JESUS

Much to his surprise, Barabbas found himself not being prepared for crucifixion, but rather taken to Pilate's hall. What was going on? Barabbas soon had his answer. He suddenly found himself standing on a balcony with Pilate and Jesus of Nazareth. Pilate was going to ask the throng gathered below to choose whether he, Barabbas, or Jesus should be released.

There was no doubt in Barabbas' mind about the outcome. The multitude would choose Jesus, and he would be on his way to a cross. The only thing this had changed was the time. He would be crucified later, but still crucified.

To his amazement, he hears the crowd crying: '… release to us Barabbas' (v. 18).

And Pilate, equally astonished, asks: 'What then do you want me to do with Him whom you call the King of the Jews?' (Mark 15:12).

And the booming answer is 'Crucify him, crucify him!' (v. 21).

Pilate turns to a soldier and says: 'Release Barabbas.' And Barabbas, who thought this would be the day of his death, finds himself a free man. The sentence has been lifted!

What did Barabbas do with himself after this stunning turn of events? Did he go to a few of his favourite 'haunts' in Jerusalem only to discover that most of the people had gone outside the city to witness the crucifixion? Did he decide to take it in as well?

And now, perhaps, he is standing there, looking at the man on the middle cross, and it hits him with sledgehammer force—he would have been there had Jesus not taken his place.

JESUS AND SINNERS

Every believer in Jesus Christ is named 'Barabbas'. As the latter was guilty of breaking the laws of the Roman government and was justly condemned to die, so we all have broken God's laws and stand justly condemned to die.

God demands perfect righteousness of each and every one of us before he will allow us to enter into eternal fellowship with him. What is perfect righteousness? It is completely complying with God's commandments. We have not met that demand. The truth is that we have broken God's laws time after time. We have broken them in thought, in word and in deed. We have failed to do those things God has commanded us to do, and we have done those things that he has commanded us not to do. We stand guilty before him!

Some wonder why God does not just ignore our sins. Why does he not just turn his head and look the other way? But

God's very nature will not allow him to do so! If God were to ignore our sin, he would deny himself.

His holy nature requires him to pronounce judgement on our sin, and judgement he has pronounced! That judgement is eternal separation from himself.

Here is the glory of the Christian gospel—the very God who has pronounced sentence upon us for our sins has made a way for us to escape that sentence. That way is his Son, Jesus.

Jesus was none other than the eternal Son of God in human flesh. He had to take our humanity in order to lift the sentence of death from us. He had to be one of us to do something for us!

In our humanity, the Lord Jesus essentially did two things. First, he lived in perfect obedience to God's holy law. While we have broken it time after time and place after place, the Lord Jesus did not break it at all. By his life, he provided the perfect righteousness that God demands, that righteousness which we do not possess.

Then the Lord Jesus went to the cross to die a special kind of death. There he received the wrath of God in the stead of all those who believe. That cross was nothing less than Jesus receiving the wrath of God in the place of sinners. Is God's sentence on our sins eternal separation from himself? On the cross, the Lord Jesus bore our eternity's worth of separation. Eternity was compressed upon him so that he bore in a short time an infinite amount of wrath. That is why he cried: 'My God, my God, why have you forsaken Me?' (Matthew 27:46).

Because Jesus received that wrath, all who believe in him do not have to receive it themselves, but are rather clothed in the righteousness of Jesus Christ.

R. A. Finlayson writes: 'Barabbas had a wonderful angle on

the cross; he could point to the middle cross and say, "There would I have been, if he had not been put in my place."'[1]

And the angle Barabbas had is the same angle that every believer has.

Note

1   Cited by **Frederick S. Leahy,** *The Cross He Bore* (Edinburgh: The Banner of Truth Trust, 1996), p. 72.

8. Those along the way

Luke 23:26–31

Simon of Cyrene and those Jesus called 'daughters of Jerusalem' (v. 28) seem to be mere window dressing for the mighty drama that is unfolding before us, the drama of Jesus' death on the cross.

But closer inspection reveals that Simon and these women have some vital lessons to share with us about the cross of Christ.

Simon of Cyrene speaks to us about:

THE DEPTH OF THE HUMILIATION OF JESUS

The humiliation of Christ is written all over the enlistment of Simon to bear the cross of Jesus. The Roman soldiers had treated Jesus in the vilest fashion imaginable. They had flogged him until the flesh of his back was a bloody mass. They had crowned him with thorns. They had spat upon him and ridiculed him.

Now, as they paraded him through the gates of the city of Jerusalem toward Golgotha, they apparently became uncertain about whether he would be able to bear his cross all the way to the crucifixion site. They found the answer to their problem in Simon. Immediately they pressed him into service, and Simon, who only a moment earlier was approaching this ghastly processional, found himself part of it.

The humiliation of Christ at this point lay, at least in part, in this: Commanding is the prerogative of one in authority, and he, Jesus, who possessed all authority in heaven and earth, stood meekly by while others exercised authority. He willingly yielded his authority.

Only a few days earlier, he had in kingly fashion secured a colt and had triumphantly ridden into the city (Luke 19:28–40). Just hours before he was condemned to death, he had secured a room to use for supper with his disciples (Luke 22:7–13). Even now as he bears his cross, he is fully aware that his commanding power is completely intact. At the very moment the soldiers were enlisting Simon, Jesus could have called twelve legions of angels from the courts of heaven and put an end to the whole business (Matthew 26:53).

He could even have required a Roman soldier to have shouldered his cross, bear it to Golgotha and die in his stead.

Why, with this power, did Jesus stand so silently and meekly as the soldiers exercised their authority? Why did he so willingly lay it aside? The answer is that he could purchase eternal redemption for sinners, not by using his kingly power to avoid the cross, but only by submitting to it.

He came to this world to die on that cross. There he would stand in the stead of sinners, receiving in his own person the penalty of God against their sins, and would, in so doing, free them from that same penalty.

If we have a true understanding of that cross, we will see that it was not the Roman soldiers who nailed Jesus to it. Yes, they did, in the sense of driving the physical nails into his hands and feet, but, in a larger sense, it was our sins that nailed him there. He went there to die for sinners. The Roman soldiers compelled Simon of Cyrene to bear the cross of Jesus. We, by our sins, compelled Jesus to bear the cross.

We don't know much about Simon of Cyrene. He strolls out of obscurity to make his brief appearance on history's stage and then returns to obscurity.

Did he resent being forced to carry this instrument of humiliation and shame? Did he glare at this one whose cross he had to bear? We do not know. What effect did carrying Jesus' cross have on Simon? Did he stay there at the site of the crucifixion to see Jesus die?

Let us nurture the hope that he did and that there on barren Golgotha he came to understand that it was not so much he that bore Jesus' cross but Jesus that bore his. Scripture gives us a hint that Simon came to embrace in true and living faith the redeeming death Jesus died there. Mark 15:21 tells us Simon was the father of Rufus. Years later the apostle Paul referred to a man named Rufus as 'a choice man in the Lord' (Romans 16:13, NASB).

Perhaps Simon did indeed come to faith that day and was enabled by the Spirit of God to lead his family to faith as well.

Whether Simon accepted Christ we cannot say with certainty, but we can say that we have in him a picture of the very essence and nature of the Christian life. Luke tells us that the soldiers laid the cross on Simon that 'he might bear it after Jesus'.

Scripture clearly teaches that all of us who embrace that instrument of Jesus' humiliation as the only hope for our salvation are not finished with it at the moment we are saved. The cross that saves is at the very heart and centre of the Christian life. Jesus himself said: 'If anyone desires to come after Me, let him deny himself, and take up his cross, and follow Me' (Matthew 16:24).

As Simon trailed along behind Jesus bearing that wooden cross, so we who are Christians are called to follow after him while bearing all the humiliation and difficulties that are part and parcel of knowing him.

That brings us to consider the lesson the daughters of Jerusalem teach us, namely:

THE DANGER OF MERE SENTIMENTALITY

Here they are weeping as Jesus takes his tortured steps to Golgotha. It was a sight that was so gruesome that any sensitive soul might well be driven to tears. The kindly and gracious Jesus, who had unleashed torrents of blessing upon so many, was now a bloody mass of humanity being herded and prodded along.

Noting their tears, Jesus did not tell them to stop weeping, but rather to make sure they were weeping for the right thing. He said they should not weep for him but rather for themselves and their children.

They were not to weep for him, because he was not on the way to the cross as just another in a long line of poor victims. He was not just another unfortunate man who had been overtaken by catastrophe. He was a man on a mission. He was on the road to the cross because he wanted to be. For this purpose he came into the world. Yes, the cross was to bring to him the most horrible suffering imaginable, but during that suffering he would be able to see those who would be saved by it and would find immense joy in their salvation (Isaiah 53:10–11; Hebrews 12:2). And that suffering would soon be over, and he would rise again and ascend to the Father in heaven.

These women, however, were to weep for themselves and their children because of what lay ahead of them. In a few short years, the Romans would come in and visit terrible destruction upon the city of Jerusalem. That day would bring untold misery and suffering upon the women and children of Jerusalem, so much so that the childless would be considered blessed, and people would yearn for the very mountains and hills to fall on them and cover them (vv. 29–30).

But, as immense and profound as that suffering would be, it would not seem to be sufficient to warrant Jesus' warning to weep for themselves and not for him. It surely would be terrible suffering, but it certainly was no greater than the suffering Jesus was to bear on the cross.

We are able to see the reason for Jesus' warning only if we take notice of his next statement: 'For if they do these things in the green wood, what will be done in the dry?' (v. 31).

With those words he was pointing them to the reality of their spiritual condition. He was a green, living tree connected to God, bearing fruit for him in the midst of his suffering and going back to him when his suffering was done.

But they were dry trees. There was no spiritual life in them and no spiritual fruit from them. And the catastrophe awaiting them in the Roman invasion would be truly catastrophic because it would plunge many of them into an eternity for which they had not prepared, an eternity in which all the spiritually dead and fruitless will be consumed by the fire of God's judgement (John 15:6).

What do the words of Jesus to these women have to do with

us? They bring us face to face with a lesson that is incredibly significant and relevant. It is fairly common these days for people to be emotionally moved by the cross without actually embracing it as their only hope for eternal salvation.

Each Easter many churches offer very lavish pageants in which the suffering of Christ is re-enacted in a very moving way. A cross is carried in, laid on the platform, and the one who is portraying Jesus is placed on that cross by the 'soldiers'.

The sound of the blows of the hammer that 'nail' the victim to the cross is most wrenching. And then that cross is hoisted up on the platform and the 'blood' is streaming down. All of this is set to incredibly moving and beautiful music. And many are so profoundly touched by it all that they cannot help but weep.

Such pageants, no matter how accurately they portray the historical details, are worse than useless if they do nothing more than cause us to weep out of sympathy over the pain and anguish Jesus endured.

We do not truly embrace the cross by weeping over Jesus' suffering there. We must rather weep over the sins—our sins—that made that suffering necessary. Furthermore, we must realize that, if we do not break with those sins and trust in Christ's redeeming death, we will be consumed by the fires of God's judgement.

Any Easter pageant that points to the suffering of Christ without making it clear why that suffering was necessary has failed.

9. Those around the cross

Matthew 27:39–44

The crucifixion of Jesus brought together a most interesting collection of individuals. The Roman soldiers were there. Utterly oblivious to the identity of the one they had affixed to the centre cross and the enormous significance of his dying there, they gave themselves to dividing his garments (vv. 33–36).

William Hendriksen describes the tragedy of these men and the ongoing tragedy they represent:

> Poor, poor soldiers! How much did they take home from Calvary? A few pieces of clothing! No truly penitent hearts, no renewed visions, no changed lives, no Saviour? Even today, how much—or how little—do some people carry home with them from the church service, the Bible class, the hymn sing, the revival meeting?[1]

Also at Jesus' crucifixion were the thieves on each side of him (v. 38) and women from Galilee (vv. 55–56). But the passers-by (vv. 39–40) and the religious leaders (vv. 41–44) now call for our attention.

Those passing by may very well have been the last of the pilgrims on their way to Jerusalem for the observance of the Passover, or they may have been on their way to some other destination. Whatever the case, they paused at the site of the crucifixion. It is interesting that they felt no need to hurl ridicule at the thieves being crucified with Jesus. Instead they centred their attention on Jesus and began to mock and ridicule him in a very malicious manner. It is not surprising that they should have stopped at the site of the crucifixion. Although death is a gory sight, we always seem to find it irresistibly riveting.

Furthermore, it is not surprising that they knew Jesus. His ministry had made him the talk of the land. But what possessed them to ridicule him? Most of us, no matter how much we dislike a man, would not ridicule him while he was dying. But these people ridiculed Jesus.

The answer to this puzzle is found in the sinful nature of man. Men are in the darkness of sin and have a natural animosity toward the light of God. The brighter the light shines, the more they hate it, and it has never shone more brightly than it did in Jesus. In degrading him, those passing by the cross showed the depth of their own degradation.

On the other hand, the religious leaders were not content merely to pause at the crucifixion site, hurl their insults and then move on. Their hatred for Jesus was so intense that they wanted to savour each ghastly detail. Each moment he suffered was delightfully delicious to them.

This mockery, as cruel as mockery can ever be, is extremely significant for each and every one of us. One point of application is obviously this: the sinful human nature that drove these men is, alas, still with us. But their mockery speaks to us at other points as well. These points emerge as we note the focus of their mockery, the irony of it, and the grand misconception that guided it.

Consider first:

THE FOCUS OF THEIR MOCKERY

Those passing by seized upon a statement Jesus had made early in his ministry. After he drove the moneychangers from the temple, Jesus was asked to provide some sort of sign to show that he had the right to do this thing. Jesus responded in this way: 'Destroy this temple, and in three days I will raise it up' (John 2:19).

He was telling them that they would have the sign they wanted when he finally arose from the grave. Completely misconstruing his words, they took him to mean that he would in three days rebuild the temple from which he had just driven the moneychangers. But he was talking about a different kind of temple, that is, the temple of his body. He was declaring that he would be raised from the grave on the third day (John 2:20–22).

Here at the cross they hurl his words back at him. Anyone who could build a temple in three days should have no trouble at all in coming down from the cross! Little did they realize that they were ridiculing and blaspheming him on the basis of a faulty understanding of his words.

They were very sure of themselves, but they were dead wrong, and the very one they were ridiculing was now only hours away from springing from the grave and fulfilling his prediction.

The religious leaders may very well have said the same thing. But they also proceeded to observe that, while he had saved others, he could not save himself (v. 42). In addition to that, they hooted at his claim to be the Son of God (v. 43). To them it was utterly ludicrous that the Son of God should be dying on the cross.

This mockery, vile as it was, happened two thousand years ago. How can something that happened so long ago have anything to do with us? Because, for one thing, the one who was crucified on that long ago day not only arose from the grave but still lives today. As he still lives, we can still mock him. One way we can do so is by refusing to submit to Scripture.

Students of the Bible know Jesus came to exercise a threefold office, that of prophet, priest and king. As priest he was to make an atonement for sinners. As king he was to rule over the hearts of his people. As prophet he was to declare the truth of God. He had done this with his statement about the temple of his body being raised on the third day. He had done it when he claimed to be the Son of God.

You see, it was Christ's exercising of his prophetic office that excited the derision of the passers-by and the religious leaders. Here is the point we need to understand: Christ has not ceased to function as prophet.

We have in Scripture the Lord Jesus Christ declaring to us the truth of God, and we are responsible for hearing and heeding that word. When we fail to do so, we are just as guilty of mocking him as if we had been on Golgotha that day and joined our voices with the passers-by and the religious leaders.

How many are doing this! Like those who passed by the cross, they are very sure of themselves and they are very quick to pronounce on Christianity. But, just as those passing by the cross did not understand what they were talking about, so these rejecters of Christianity haven't the foggiest notion of what they are rejecting.

A second aspect of this mockery that makes it so significant is:

THE IRONY OF THEIR MOCKERY

The irony is this: The very mockery these men used to dispute Christ's claim constituted a proof of the same.

This mockery was a fulfilment of centuries-old prophecies. The 22nd Psalm is such a detailed and precise prophecy of Christ's crucifixion that it seems almost to have been written by one who was standing at the foot of the cross. David, the author of the psalm, writes:

> But I am a worm, and no man;
>> A reproach of men, and despised by the people.
> All those who see Me ridicule Me;
>> They shoot out the lip, they shake the head, saying,
> He trusted in the LORD, let him rescue Him;
>> Let him deliver Him, since He delights in Him!'
>
>> (Psalm 22:6–8).

It should be noted that the mockery on Golgotha is only one prophecy Jesus fulfilled. There are many, many more. One count puts the total at 325. All of these fulfilled prophecies leave us no room to manoeuvre. They make it overwhelmingly clear that Jesus was exactly who he claimed to be: God in human flesh. While the mockers gleefully concluded Jesus could not be the Son of God, he was demonstrating that he was.

Those of us who believe we have eternal salvation through

this crucified Christ often find ourselves enduring mockery even as our Christ did. Those who mock tend to think we hold this faith for no reason, that it amounts to nothing more than a vain superstition that has been passed down from generation to generation. The prophecies Christ fulfilled in his birth, life and death remind all of us who know the Lord that we have solid grounds for our faith. And those same prophecies invite unbelievers to suspend their mockery long enough to consider the evidence for Christ.

That brings us to another aspect:

THE GRAND MISCONCEPTION BEHIND THEIR MOCKERY

Look again at what the passers-by and the religious leaders said to Jesus. What did they assume as they hurled their insults at him? There is no difficulty here. They assumed it was weakness that kept Jesus on the cross, that he was, after all, a mere man and could not come down from the cross although he desperately desired to do so.

They could not have been more wrong. It was not weakness that held Jesus there but strength such as had never been known before. Jesus himself said he could have called twelve legions of angels from heaven to deliver him from the cross (Matthew 26:53).

See the angels now standing at the borders of heaven and strapping on their swords. In awe they watch as their Master is nailed to the cross. They watch as that cross is dropped into the ground. They watch as the mockers come by the cross. Any moment now the Master will call and they will put an end to the whole wretched business. But the call does not come. The immortal dies!

Oh wonderful the wonders left undone!
And scarce less wonderful than those he wrought;
Oh self-restraint, passing all human thought,
To have all power, and be as having none;
Oh self-denying love, which felt alone
For needs of others, never for its own

(R. C. Trench).

The angels must have been mystified by it all, but we who have trusted in Christ understand. We understand that it was not the nails that held Jesus to the cross. It was his love for sinners. Had he come down from that cross, there would have been no redemption for us. He had to die there, taking the penalty we deserve so there would be no penalty left for us to pay.

Let unbelievers and the very demons of hell mock and disdain. We who are saved will for ever adore.

Note

1 **William Hendriksen,** *New Testament Commentary: Luke* (Grand Rapids: Baker Book House, 1978), p. 1029.

10. Those on the outer crosses

Luke 23:39–43

In these verses Luke sets before us in plain and powerful language two more men who were associated with the cross of Christ: the thieves crucified with him. It should not escape our attention that the presence of these two men fulfilled the prophecy of Isaiah 53:12: '... he was numbered with the transgressors'.

These two men speak to us at the point of our greatest need. They speak to us about this matter of eternal salvation.

One thief speaks to us about:

THE POSSIBILITY OF FALLING SHORT OF ETERNAL LIFE

What a dreadful and frightening sight we have in this man! He is at most only a hair's breadth away from being plunged into eternity, and eternal life, if we may say so, was nothing more than a few feet away. But he missed it! So close and yet so very far!

How do we know that this man missed out on eternal life? The answer is very simple. The Lord Jesus spoke these precious words to the other thief: 'Assuredly, I say to you, today you will be with Me in Paradise' (v. 43).

But he spoke those words to the one thief only. The thief we are now considering did not hear those words spoken to him. They could have been, but they were not.

What a powerful message there is here! We have come upon a day in which most people seem to fancy that all will be well with them in eternity regardless of what they do with Christ. They can, to their way of thinking, join the thief who repented, and be saved. Or they can go to their graves completely disregarding Christ and his claims, as the other thief did, and still be saved.

But this is a delusion from hell itself. One thief heard the promise of Christ, but the other did not. Let us learn from this that all are not automatically saved.

But let's turn our attention to another question. How is it that this one malefactor missed out on eternal life? How did this unspeakable tragedy come about?

Luke tells us this man 'blasphemed' Christ by saying: 'If You are the Christ, save Yourself and us' (v. 39).

It is obvious that this man picked up on what others were saying in their mockery of Christ. The Roman soldiers (vv. 36–37), the passers-by (Matthew 27:39–40) and the religious leaders (Matthew 27:41–43) essentially challenged the Lord to prove he was the Son of God by coming down from the cross.

In their mockery, this thief saw a glimmer of hope. In all likelihood he had heard of Jesus and the astonishing miracles that he had performed. Perhaps he did possess the power to come down from that cross and he could be taunted into exercising that power! But, notice, the thief was not interested so much in Jesus proving that he was the Son of God by coming down from the cross as he was in Jesus including him.

As we ponder his words, it becomes apparent to us that this

life was everything to him and must be tenaciously held. He saw in Jesus a way to cling to this life. His only interest in Jesus was as a means to get what he, the thief, wanted. He had no interest in being part of Christ's plan but rather wanted Christ to adopt his plan, namely, escaping from the cross so life in this world could be continued.

This man died a short time after hurling his blasphemy at Christ, but his error has not died. There are still multitudes who have no interest at all in the spiritual kingdom that the Lord Jesus came to establish. They are not interested in breaking with their sins and receiving him as their Saviour. They are certainly not interested in living under his Lordship and obeying his commands.

Their only interest in Christ is as a 'ticket'. When they are sick, they want to use him as their ticket to health. When they have financial reversals, they want Christ to be their ticket to prosperity. When their family begins to fall apart, they want Christ to be their ticket to domestic tranquility. They do not want Christ to rule and reign over them. They are not interested in serving him. They want him to serve them. This life is everything to them, even as it was to this thief, and they desire a troubleshooter Christ who will jump when life gets tough and smooth everything out.

The second thief presents us with a far different picture. Here is:

THE POSSIBILITY OF RECEIVING ETERNAL LIFE

This man, unlike the first thief, did not miss out on eternal life. As his life faded away, he saw the door of eternal glory open before him.

Scripture tells us that this man at first joined with his fellow-thief in reviling Jesus (Matthew 27:44; Mark 15:32).

But this second thief did not long continue with his mockery. There was something about Jesus that arrested him. He realized that Jesus was not in the same category as he and the other thief, that Jesus was not even in the same category as other men. As his life ebbed away, this thief realized that Jesus was in fact the Son of God and the only hope for eternal salvation. So he cried out to Jesus: 'Lord, remember me when You come into Your kingdom' (v. 42).

The Lord Jesus responded to this prayer with these blessed words: 'Assuredly, I say to you, today you will be with me in Paradise' (v. 43).

Those words have a world of meaning tucked into them.

HEAVEN IS A REAL PLACE

First, they tell us there is a glorious state, a glorious condition beyond this life. Jesus here calls it Paradise. What was he talking about? Only two other times do we find this word used in Scripture (2 Corinthians 12:4; Revelation 2:7), and in each case it is used as a synonym for heaven.

Jesus was, therefore, promising life in heaven to this thief, and this promise was going to be fulfilled that very day. The moment that thief died his soul went immediately into the presence of God. His body was, of course, taken down from the cross, and, we presume, buried. When the Lord Jesus Christ comes again, that body will be raised from the grave and will be reunited with his soul. But the soul of that thief joined God in heaven on the day he died. It remains in heaven today, and it will remain there until the day of the resurrection.

Heaven! What a glorious thought! And we may rest assured that our greatest flights of imagination fall far short of the reality. No tears. No sorrow. No pain. No death. No parting. Isn't it amazing that so few are interested in this place and how to get there?

JESUS HAS THE KEYS TO HEAVEN

The second thing the words of Jesus tell us is that he is the One who has the keys to heaven.

The thief called him 'Lord'. Here Jesus was dying on a cross and this man called him 'Lord'. He didn't look like God in human flesh at that point, but the Spirit of God had so worked faith in the thief's heart that he was able to look beyond outward appearances to see the reality of who Jesus was. So it is today. When the Spirit of God works faith in a person's heart he enables that person to see what others can't see.

Notice that Jesus did not dispute what the man had said or correct him. When this man said 'Lord', Jesus simply responded in lordly fashion by saying: 'I say to you' (v. 43). So he accepted the title the thief used for him!

Here's the point. If Jesus is Lord, he has supreme authority over all, including entrance to Paradise.

THOSE FOR WHOM JESUS USES THE KEYS

The third thing the words of Jesus tell us is what we must do if we want the Lord to open heaven's door to us.

Let's not forget that Jesus spoke these words in response to what this thief had prayed. What did this thief's prayer include? It contains, in the words of one commentator, 'a very large and long creed'.[1]

In effect, the thief said the following: 'I am a sinful man. I deserve the punishment placed upon me. This man, on the other hand, is pure and righteous. I will, therefore, trust him and him alone for my salvation.'

Would you have heaven's door swing open to you? Would you enter Paradise? You must make the prayer of this thief yours. You must stop arguing with God and start agreeing with him. You must say the same thing about yourself that God says about you, namely, that you are indeed a sinner and deserving only of his eternal wrath. You must further recognize that you can do no more to help yourself than this thief could do. You must see that Jesus Christ is your only hope for salvation and cast yourself entirely on his mercy and grace.

It was not an accident that Jesus' cross was placed between the two thieves. He is the great divider of men. Those who receive him are saved; those who reject him are for ever lost. Those two thieves, one on Jesus' right and the other on his left, are not only fitting symbols for all humanity this very day, but also for that future day of judgement when his sheep will be placed on his right and the goats will be placed on his left and driven away for ever.

Where do you stand in relationship to Christ? If you are on the wrong side of Christ, you must act quickly and decisively. Flee to him as the penitent thief did. Those who go through life on the wrong side of Christ will certainly find themselves on the wrong side of him in eternity.

Perhaps you recognize that you are on the wrong side of Christ and you intend to do something about it, but not today. Perhaps you fancy that you can turn to Christ at the last minute as the penitent thief did. This is a grave mistake. Death may so quickly snatch you away that you have no opportunity to repent. The course of wisdom is to repent today. There is great truth in the point that has been so frequently made—one thief was saved, so no one need despair; but only one, so no one should dare to presume.

Notes

1 **J. C. Ryle,** *Expository Thoughts on the Gospels: Luke* (Edinburgh: The Banner of Truth Trust, 1986), vol. ii, p. 476.

11. John and Mary[1]

John 19:25–27

Jesus spoke seven times while he was on the cross. The third of these 'words' reveals his heart of love for those who have already come to know him. The people of God are always divided into two groups: those who have not yet come to know Christ, and those who have. The love of Christ goes out to each of these.

Who can comprehend the tender love Christ has for his own? The apostle John, in his introduction of the night before Jesus was crucified, gives us a glimpse of that love with these words: 'Now before the Feast of the Passover, when Jesus knew that His hour had come that He should depart from this world to the Father, having loved His own who were in the world, He loved them to the end' (John 13:1).

It would have been a marvel that Jesus should have felt even a fleeting compassion for anyone in this world of sin. But Jesus did not feel a fleeting compassion for one. He had an abiding love for the many John refers to as 'his own'.

John gives us another glimpse into the love of Christ for his own with the third word Jesus spoke from the cross.

'Now there stood by the cross of Jesus His mother ...' (v. 25). Are there any words more heart-wrenching than these? Jesus was dying the most horrid, ignominious death possible and his mother was there to see it. She heard the hammer blows that drove the nails, and winced with each blow. She saw the cruel cross lifted in the air and heard his cry of pain as it was dropped abruptly into the ground. She saw the blood streaming down. She heard the mockery and ridicule of the gloating religious leaders and the others around the cross. She heard the callous cursing and laughing of the soldiers as they went about their grim business.

Shortly after Jesus was born that old saint of God, Simeon, looked deep into Mary's eyes and somberly said: '... yes, a sword will pierce through your own soul also ...' (Luke 2:35).

There in the shadow of the cross Mary felt the thrust of that sword. Never were a more gruesome death and a more gracious Son joined as here.

The other women gathered there around the cross had probably tried to persuade her to move away from the savage spectacle, but she was inexorably drawn there by one of the strongest forces known to man—a mother's love. 'Many waters cannot quench love, Nor can the floods drown it' (Song of Solomon 8:7).

We are blessed if, when the trials of life swell up around us, we have faithful friends on whom we can depend to the very end. These Mary had. Her sister was there. And Mary Magdalene, that woman who owed such a massive debt to grace, was there. And one of the twelve, John, was there.

All of Jesus' disciples had forsaken him and fled, but John had returned. John consistently identifies himself in this Gospel as 'the disciple whom Jesus loved'. Perhaps that phrase carries with it the reason he thought better of his cowardice and returned to take his place at the foot of the cross. The glory of his life was in being embraced by the love of Christ. No, he didn't glory in his love for Christ. It was too weak and faltering.

PEOPLE IN THE PASSION OF JESUS

But the love of Christ for him! That must have been the invisible hand that pulled him back to his rightful place. If we are to shun cowardice and stand with Christ as John did, we must dwell much on the Christ who loved us and gave himself for us.

That little company of believers must have felt very much alone there on that barren Golgotha. They were a tiny island of love and devotion in a sea of hatred and disdain. They were a tiny patch of blue in a sullen, grey sky. They were a spray of tender flowers in the midst of a tangle of thorns and brambles. Suddenly Jesus looked upon that little company and spoke to his mother: 'Woman, behold your son.' He must have nodded towards John as he spoke those words.

And then to John, he said: 'Behold your mother', and nodded towards Mary.

These few words carried a world of meaning for Mary, and they contain powerful and large lessons for us.

JESUS' TENDER CONCERN FOR THE NEEDS OF THIS LIFE

First, they show us the tender concern of the Lord Jesus for those who have pressing, urgent needs in this life.

Mary had such needs. The future must have looked very bleak to her as she stood there watching her son die. Her husband had died. Her other sons had still not accepted Jesus as the Messiah, and she probably couldn't count on them for either physical or emotional support. And now Jesus was being taken from her.

What was to become of her? Jesus' words gave the answer. With those words he placed Mary in John's care and charged John to treat her as though she were his own mother. His words found their mark for the next thing we read is: '… from that hour that disciple took her to his own home'.

PEOPLE IN THE PASSION OF JESUS

So Jesus was not so occupied with his own needs that he neglected the needs of his mother. He saw to it that she was cared for before he died.

Concern for others was always in the forefront of Jesus' life, and now it is foremost in his death. The first three words of Jesus from the cross were spoken on behalf of others.

This isn't surprising. The whole purpose of Jesus' death was to help others. He didn't have to die. No Roman nails were strong enough to hold him to that cross. He died for our sake and the nails that held him there were the nails of love. He was there to act as our High Priest, to make an atonement for sin, and to offer it to God on the behalf of his people.

There are a couple of things for us to learn from Jesus' concern for the needs of others. First, if Jesus is so deeply concerned about our needs, we can and should bring our needs to him. What troubles you today? Have friends turned against you? Do you carry serious illness in your body? Are you lonely and depressed? No matter what your problem is and no matter how overwhelming it is, there are two things you should do. First, think long and hard on these precious words from the author of Hebrews: 'For we do not have a High Priest who cannot sympathize with our weaknesses' (Hebrews 4:15). Then do as the hymn-writer says and take your burden to Jesus:

> I must tell Jesus all of my trials;
> I cannot bear these burdens alone;
> In my distress he kindly will help me;
> He ever loves and cares for his own   (Elisha A. Hoffman).

Thank God, we can bring our burdens to Jesus with the

confidence that he cares about us and will help us. That doesn't necessarily mean he will remove the burden from us. If he doesn't we may rest assured it is because the burden is for our good and he will give us strength and grace to bear it.

Jesus' concern for the needs of others teaches another lesson as well. If our Lord was so concerned about others, his followers should also be concerned about others.

Have we learned this lesson from our Lord? Or have we bought into the self-centredness of our day? How much do we really live for others and care for their needs? Their needs, problems, wants, circumstances and disappointments make up all of reality as far as many are concerned.

Let's see to it that we never forget that our family members are included in that category of 'others'. Often we treat the worst those we profess to love the most.

In particular, let's make sure we obey God's clear command to honour our parents. If Jesus had time in the midst of dying to respect his mother, we can surely find time in the midst of living to respect our parents.

What does it mean to respect our parents? It means giving them obedience in our younger years, support in their older years, and respect through all their years.

THE PRIORITY OF THE NEXT LIFE

The second significant lesson these words teach us is the priority Jesus gives to preparing for the next life.

This lesson comes out in a couple of ways.

JESUS' COMMITMENT TO THE CROSS

First, the fact that Jesus was concerned about Mary and her

physical needs didn't cause him to come down from the cross and abandon the work of redemption he was performing there. He could have done this. He didn't have to stay on the cross. He could have put Mary's physical needs above everything else and come down from the cross, but he didn't. Instead he gave priority to opening the door of heaven to all who believe in him.

THE WAY IN WHICH JESUS ADDRESSED MARY

The second indication that Jesus gave priority to the next life arises from the way in which he addressed Mary. He doesn't address her as 'mother' but simply as 'woman'. Many have found this to be quite disturbing. It appears to them that Jesus was being rude and inconsiderate.

Nothing could be further from the truth. Jesus addressed Mary as 'woman' not to be rude but to underscore a most vital truth, namely, their relationship was now for ever changed. Herschel Ford explains it in this way:

> On the cross Jesus actually broke the relationship of mother and son. He turned her away from himself by saying, 'From now on not I, but John, is to be your son.' From that time he is no longer anyone's son—he is the world's Saviour. Mary no longer is the mother, she is a simple believer, and her Son has become her Saviour … He provided for her as a Saviour a million times better home than he provided for her as a son.[2]

F. W. Krummacher makes the same point in these words:

> His earthly connection with her must give way to a superior one. As though he had said, 'Thou, my mother, wilt from this time be as one

of my daughters, and I thy Lord ... The relationships according to the flesh and the manner of the world have an end; other and more spiritual and heavenly take their place.'[3]

It's surely not an accident that we find Jesus using the same form of address for Mary on another occasion when he was much occupied with the work of the cross (John 2:4).

While Jesus was concerned about Mary's physical needs, he was even more concerned about carrying out the work of providing eternal salvation for sinners. The needs of this life pale in comparison to that.

Have you received the eternal life Jesus came to provide? Many seem only to be interested in the Christ of the physical needs. They want a God who cares about them in the here and now, and who helps them with the problems of this life, but they disdain the eternal salvation he offers. They want to accept the lesser gift of his caring concern for the problems of this life, and reject the greater gift of eternal life. The tragedy is that they can have both.

Notes

1 I have written similar thoughts in *Journey to the Cross* (Darlington: Evangelical Press, 1997), pp. 169–74.

2 **Herschel Ford,** *Seven Simple Sermons* (Grand Rapids: Zondervan, 1945), pp. 38–9.

3 **F. W. Krummacher,** *The Suffering Savior* (Grand Rapids: Kregel Publications, 1992), p. 373.

PEOPLE IN THE PASSION OF JESUS

12. The soldiers and the centurion

Matthew 27:27–31, 35, 50–54

T hese verses show us two possibilities on the vital matter of receiving the eternal life provided by the Lord Jesus Christ. These possibilities, represented so long ago by the Roman soldiers and their commander, are still with us.

THE POSSIBILITY OF MISSING OUT WHILE PLAYING AROUND

The Bible has its share of tragic figures. We have noticed some in this series: Caiaphas and Judas. Many other names come quickly to mind: Cain, Esau, Lot, Achan, King Saul.

I do not hesitate to add to the list the men we find in the verses of our text—the Roman soldiers who crucified Jesus. These men were at first oblivious to the earth-shaking significance of the crucifixion of Jesus. They were connected with the greatest event in all of human history, and they did not realize it.

Their tragedy goes even deeper. It is not just that they were oblivious to the realities unfolding around them. They were also absorbed with the trivial while it was going on! While Jesus was being crucified, they gambled for his garments. While Jesus was on the cross to provide a garment of eternal righteousness for all who would believe, these men were content to gamble for garments that would soon pass away.

They missed out on the greatest thing that ever happened because they were playing around. Missing out while playing around!

Why do you suppose the Holy Spirit, the author of Scripture, saw to it that these soldiers were included in the historical record? After all, we are dealing with very few minutes here. Jesus was on the cross from nine in the morning until three in the afternoon, a total of 360 minutes. How many minutes did it take for the soldiers to gamble for his garments? Not many! Why, then, did the Holy Spirit want this included?

While the gambling of the soldiers represents only a brief point in time, it is found at every point in time. The gambling of those soldiers was fleeting and temporary, but that which is represented by it is ongoing, namely, being so occupied with the trivial that we are oblivious to gigantic spiritual truths swirling all around.

THE POSSIBILITY OF FINDING REAL FAITH

The Gospel accounts contain several ringing confessions of faith: Nathanael's (John 1:49), Simon Peter's (Matthew 16:16; John 6:68–69), Thomas' (John 20:28), and the disciples' (Matthew 14:33).

Included in this company is the sparkling confession of faith that came from the man at the foot of the cross, the Roman centurion.

In some ways, this is the most marvellous confession of all. The others came from disciples of Jesus. These were men informed by the promises of God in the Old Testament and were nurtured with anticipation of a coming Messiah; but this centurion was not in this company. He was a pagan Gentile. At best, he was meagrely informed concerning the truths God had revealed to the nation of Israel. He had gods of his own, gods he could see and touch.

Furthermore, as a veteran in this sorry business of crucifixion, he was certainly not inclined to believe that a crucified man could be the Son of God. The Romans reserved crucifixion for the very dregs of society.

This man was not, therefore, in any way predisposed to making such a confession, but, marvel of marvels, here we find him saying: 'Truly this was the Son of God!' (v. 54).

This confession leads us to raise a couple of questions about the centurion.

ON WHAT BASIS DID HE MAKE HIS CONFESSION?

Was his confession due to a mere passing whim? Or was it on the basis of solid evidence? We must say it was the latter. The centurion was confronted with evidence that could not be denied.

We cannot say with certainty how long this centurion had been directly involved with Jesus. We assume that he was present when the soldiers under his command mocked and scourged Jesus and wove a crown of thorns for his head. He was certainly on hand when his soldiers led Jesus from Jerusalem to Golgotha and nailed him to the cross. He was there as his own soldiers, the passers-by, the religious leaders and the thieves hurled insults and blasphemy toward Jesus. He may have even joined with them in this cruel mockery.

While all this was going on this centurion could not help but notice the quiet dignity with which Jesus suffered.

Then there were the first words Jesus spoke from the cross: 'Father, forgive them, for they do not know what they do' (Luke 23:34).

Other men would have snarled at their crucifiers and longed for their own destruction, but not Jesus.

The centurion must also have heard those words Jesus spoke to one of the thieves: 'Assuredly, I say to you, today you will be with Me in Paradise' (Luke 23:43).

Perhaps those words set him to thinking. How could this one who was suffering such intense pain be concerned about someone else? What authority did he have to promise eternal life to a dying thief? Who was this man on this centre cross?

Then came the darkness. It was a darkness such as no one had seen before. William Hendriksen calls it 'intense and unforgettable'.[1]

This was not momentary, fleeting darkness. It began at high noon and continued for three hours. It was deep, unrelenting and profound.

Perhaps it seemed to the centurion that the very sun refused to look upon such a horrid spectacle as the crucifixion of this man on the middle cross. Perhaps at that point he could have understood these lines:

I asked the heavens, 'What foe
to God hath done
this unexampled deed?'
The heavens exclaim
''Twas man; and we in horror
snatched the sun
from such a spectacle of guilt and shame'.[2]

PEOPLE IN THE PASSION OF JESUS

The fields around Bethlehem were bathed in light when Jesus was born (Luke 2:9). It was only fitting that they should be. Jesus was the Son of God and God was with him.

But here on Golgotha impenetrable darkness falls because God has withdrawn from Jesus. The proof of this is Jesus' cry: 'My God, my God, why have You forsaken Me?' (v. 46).

On that cross Jesus became sin for his people, and the price of sin is separation from God. Jesus was separated from his Father so all who believe in him will never have to be.

After crying out again, Jesus died (v. 50). The greatest life ever lived now ended with the greatest death ever died. And to signal the significance of this death, a great earthquake rumbled through the land. The veil in the temple was torn from top to bottom—a powerful indication that the death of Jesus ended the sacrificial system of the Old Testament and opened the way to God. And the graves of some of the saints were opened and these saints were raised from the dead. They appeared briefly in Jerusalem before being received, we assume, into heaven (vv. 51–53).

The centurion, standing at the foot of the cross, did not know the veil in the temple had been rent and that people had been raised from the dead.

But the earthquake furnished for him the crowning touch on a whole series of evidences. The manner in which Jesus had conducted himself, the words which he spoke, the darkness over the land—all indicated that Jesus was no ordinary man. And now this powerful earthquake at the precise moment of his death! It all converged upon the centurion with such power that he could not lightly dismiss it. He had to admit that Jesus was indeed the Son of God. We also have reason to believe that

PEOPLE IN THE PASSION OF JESUS

the very soldiers who at first were occupied with Jesus' garments were as convinced as their commander (v. 54).

While the evidence the centurion had witnessed was powerful and convincing, it was small compared to the evidence we have. The centurion did not know about all the promises of the Old Testament and how Jesus fulfilled them. We do. The centurion may have heard some of what Jesus did during his earthly ministry. We know much of what Jesus did. The centurion came to faith at the feet of the crucified Jesus. We know that the crucified Jesus soon became the resurrected Jesus. The centurion came to faith without knowing how this crucified Jesus would change history, but we have two thousand years of history, years that are replete with changed lives.

WAS HIS CONFESSION GENUINE?

Some argue that we must not accept the words of this centurion as a full-fledged confession of faith, that he was only paying tribute to Jesus as an unusual and extraordinary man.

I do not doubt for one moment that the centurion's words came from the heart of one who had been touched by the grace of God.

We must remember that this business of salvation is not man's work but God's. It is to me unthinkable that God should allow his Son to die on that cross without immediately accomplishing the end for which that death was designed, namely, the salvation of sinners.

The fact that one of the thieves received Christ there on Golgotha pictures for us one aspect of Jesus' death. This man was presumably a Jew, and Jesus' death was certainly for the Jews.

PEOPLE IN THE PASSION OF JESUS

But, thank God, the redeeming death of Jesus was not limited to the Jewish nation. It was also intended for the Gentiles. It is to be expected, therefore, that right there on Golgotha that part of Jesus' death would be signalled in some way. If that centurion and his soldiers came to faith there at the feet of Jesus, they constituted the firstfruits of the vast harvest that was to be secured among the Gentiles.

I urge, therefore, that we not only regard the confession of this centurion as a genuine confession of faith, but that we also see in it what we ourselves must do if we are to have eternal life. We must confess the truth about Jesus. We must acknowledge that he was the Son of God, that he was nothing less than God in human flesh.

What a marvel! God here upon this earth in our humanity! What is the explanation for this? Why would God come to us in our own humanity? The answer is right there on that cross. Because of our sins, we deserve the darkness of being for ever separated from God. But Jesus took the place of sinners there on the cross. There he died in their stead. Deity cannot die, but humanity can. Jesus took our humanity, then, that he might die in that humanity, and in dying free us from our sin and condemnation.

When we truly confess from our hearts that Jesus is indeed the Son of God, we are confessing at the same time the truths of his deity and his humanity and his redeeming death in that humanity.

The centurion was not a theologian, but we can believe that an elemental understanding of these truths was born in his heart that day. We may also believe that the passing of time increased his awareness of those truths and his rejoicing in them.

If we do not see in the darkness of Calvary the Son of God dying in our stead, we will have to endure the darkness of eternal wrath ourselves. There are no other options.

Have we with our mountains of evidence for Christ joined the centurion in his confession of faith? Or are we, like the gambling soldiers, missing out on eternal life because we are occupied with mere trivialities?

Notes

1 **William Hendriksen,** *Luke* (Grand Rapids: Baker Book House, 1978), p. 1034.
2 Cited by **Frederick Leahy,** *The Cross He Bore* (Edinburgh: Banner of Truth Trust, 1996), p. 74.

13. Jesus

1 Corinthians 15:3–5, 20–23

T he greatest person associated with the Passion of Jesus was, of course, Jesus himself. Why should we be interested in Jesus? Christians do not hesitate to assert that knowing him is the most important and crucial of all matters. Why do we insist upon this?

Paul's words to the Corinthians enable us to answer. Here the apostle Paul asserts some mighty truths about Christ, truths that obviously separate Christ from all others and make knowing him vitally important.

First, Paul affirms that:

CHRIST DIED FOR SINNERS (V. 3)

He writes to his fellow believers in the church of Corinth: 'Christ died for our sins according to the Scriptures' (v. 3).

All of us who know the Lord understand that we are saved because the Lord Jesus Christ died in our stead. On the cross, he received the penalty our sins deserve, and because Jesus took that penalty there is none left for us to pay.

We understand that we are not saved because of any good thing we have done or can ever do, but rather because of the doing of the Lord Jesus Christ on our behalf. His death was substitutionary in nature. He did not die for his own sins. He had none for which to die (1 John 3:5)! He rather died for the sins of his people. On the cross, he endured the pangs of hell so those people will never have to worry about enduring those pangs themselves. He was separated from God the Father so they will never have to endure that separation.

Christians rest their hope for forgiveness of sins, standing before God and eternal glory in heaven squarely, completely and unreservedly on the death of the Lord Jesus Christ. And they are happy to trumpet the good news that the death Jesus died is sufficient for all who break with their sins and cast themselves in faith on him. Happily, there is a 'whoever' in the Bible (Revelation 22:17).

It is absolutely vital and crucial for all to come to Christ because of his death. It was a death like no other.

Paul also affirms that:

CHRIST AROSE FROM THE GRAVE (V. 4)

It's interesting that the apostle doesn't move immediately from Christ's dying to his rising from the dead. Between those powerful assertions, he inserts this statement: 'he was buried' (v. 4).

Paul wanted to make sure that his readers understood that Jesus was a real man who died a real death. There could be no doubt about this. When his body was removed from the cross, his disciples took it and prepared it for burial. They wrapped his body in linen, sprinkling spices on the linen as they wrapped.

Those disciples so extensively and thoroughly handled the body of Jesus as they prepared it for burial that they knew he was really dead. He wasn't faking it. There was no life in that body at all.

PEOPLE IN THE PASSION OF JESUS

Only if we appreciate the reality of Jesus' death can we truly appreciate the significance of what Paul says next: 'he rose again the third day' (v. 4).

That body, so obviously and completely dead, did not stay that way. The Lord Jesus Christ broke the bonds of death on the third day. He arose from the grave, never to die again.

Paul's mighty assertion gives rise to two questions of immense importance.

HOW CAN WE KNOW FOR SURE THAT JESUS AROSE FROM THE GRAVE?

How do we know this was not just a clever fabrication by his disciples?

The apostle, knowing that question would invariably surge to the forefront of the thinking of his readers, quickly moved to give them the impressive evidence for the resurrection of Christ. Cephas, the twelve, a gathering of five hundred, James, all the apostles, and Paul himself had all encountered the risen Lord (vv. 5–8).

The appearances of the risen Christ to his disciples constitute only one evidence for his resurrection. Paul could have also written of the empty tomb, the peculiar configuration of the linen strips in which Jesus' body had been wrapped, the presence of angels at the tomb, the removal of the heavy stone from the mouth of the sepulchre and the immediate transformation of the disciples from whimpering cowards to bold witnesses. All of these and more constitute a veritable avalanche of evidence that Jesus' resurrection is no mere figment of the imagination or product of wishful thinking. We regularly accept the truth of many events in history on the basis of a lot less evidence!

SO WHAT?

Many who admit the truth of Jesus' resurrection seem to wonder what all the fuss is about. They acknowledge the fact of the resurrection, but they fail to see the implications of it. They want politely to tip their hats to it and then go on their way as if it had never happened.

The apostle Paul loved to bask in the glorious implications of the resurrection of Jesus. In his epistle to the Romans, he insists that the resurrection means that Jesus is without doubt the person he claimed to be: the Son of God (Romans 1:4).

In that same letter, Paul says we have justification, that is, right standing before God, because of the resurrection of Jesus from the grave (Romans 4:25).

What is the link between Jesus' resurrection and our eternal salvation? William Hendriksen provides the answer in these words: 'The Father, by raising Jesus from the dead, assures us that the atoning sacrifice has been accepted; hence, our sins are forgiven.'[1]

Martyn Lloyd-Jones explains it in this way:

> The resurrection is the proclamation of the fact that God is fully and completely satisfied with the work that his Son did upon the cross ... If God had not raised him from the grave we might draw the conclusion that our Lord was not able to bear the punishment of the guilt of our sins, that it was too much for him, and that his death was the end.[2]

In this fifteenth chapter of 1 Corinthians, the same apostle unfolds yet another glorious implication of Christ's resurrection, namely, the resurrection unto eternal glory of all those who know him as Lord and Saviour. Paul writes: 'For as in Adam all die, even so in Christ all shall be made alive' (v. 22).

Jesus' resurrection is the guarantee of the resurrection of his disciples. On the night before he was crucified, the Lord Jesus gave this promise to his disciples: 'Because I live, you will live also' (John 14:19).

In other words, the resurrection of Jesus means that death will not have the final word in the life of Christians. When a Christian dies, his or her soul goes immediately into the presence of the Lord while his or her body goes into the grave. But the body of the believer will not stay in that grave. A day is coming in which the grave will have to give up its prey. On that day the bodies of all believers will be raised from their graves, and those bodies will be instantaneously changed into bodies like the body the Lord Jesus himself had when he came out of the grave (Philippians 3:20–21; 1 John 3:2).

When will this happen? The answer to that question brings us to yet another reason why it is so very important for each of us to know the Lord Jesus Christ, that is:

CHRIST IS COMING AGAIN (V. 23)
The apostle Paul says Christians will be 'made alive … at His coming' (vv. 22–23).

After the Lord Jesus Christ arose from the grave, he spent forty days with his disciples. During that time, he gave them 'many infallible proofs' of his resurrection (Acts 1:3).

Then the day came for him to depart from them. While they were assembled together with him on the Mount of Olives outside Jerusalem, 'He was taken up, and a cloud received Him out of their sight' (Acts 1:9).

As they stared wistfully at that spot at which they had last seen him, two men in white apparel stood by them and said: 'Men of Galilee, why do you stand gazing up into heaven? This same Jesus, who was taken up from you into heaven, will so come in like manner as you saw Him go into heaven' (Acts 1:10–11).

That day the church began to wait for her Lord to return and she began proclaiming his gospel while she waited. The waiting and the proclaiming continues. The fact that the wait has been so long does not mean that the Lord Jesus has forgotten his promise. He still lives, and, when the time is right, he will break forth from the clouds, heaven's trumpet will sound, the archangel will shout, and then the bodies of all Christians will be raised to eternal glory. And those Christians who are alive at that time will be caught up to meet them in the air (1 Thessalonians 4:13–18).

What a day it will be! But the glories of that day will be reserved for those who know the Lord. The Bible has nothing glorious to say about unbelievers. For them it uses language of unspeakable woe. Those who would share in the glory of that coming day and escape the woe must receive the Christ who died on the cross, arose from the grave and is coming again to claim his own.

Notes

1 **William Hendriksen**, *New Testament Commentary: Romans* (Grand Rapids: Baker Book House, 1980), p. 161.

2 **D. M. Lloyd-Jones**, *Romans: An Exposition of Chapters 3:20–4:25* (Grand Rapids: Zondervan, 1971), p. 144.

PEOPLE IN THE PASSION OF JESUS

PEOPLE IN THE PASSION OF JESUS

Face2face with Samuel— Encountering the king-maker

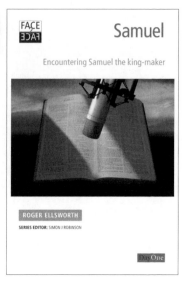

ROGER ELLSWORTH

128PP, PAPERBACK

ISBN 978–1–84625–039–2

Welcome to the world of dirt roads and oxcarts, cattle and sheep, sandals and robes! Welcome to the world of Samuel—one of the most important men in the history of the nation of Israel. Samuel was a great prophet occupying a unique position in the history of his nation. For a long time, Israel had been ruled by 'judges', but Samuel ushered them into a new era in which they were governed by kings. However, we are not taking this 'face2face' look at Samuel because we are interested in his historical uniqueness but rather because he can help us to know the God who made us and who has a wonderful purpose for all who live for him.

Roger Ellsworth has served as pastor of Immanuel Baptist Church, Benton, Illinois, for eighteen years. He is the author of twenty-seven books, including *Opening up Philippians* and *Opening up Psalms*.

'Roger Ellsworth's book is an extremely relevant and helpful study in the life of Samuel, a much-neglected Old Testament character. It is an extremely practical, pastoral and, most important of all, Christ-exalting-character study at its best and an invaluable addition to a promising series.'

DEREK PRIME

PEOPLE IN THE PASSION OF JESUS

Face2face with Elijah— Encountering Elijah the fiery prophet

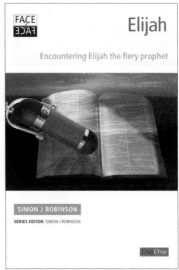

SIMON J ROBINSON

80PP, PAPERBACK

ISBN 978–1–84625–011–8

Elijah, the fiery prophet, lived in a time of intense spiritual darkness. People were openly disobeying God's commands, and true worship seemed to have been all but snuffed out. And yet God was still at work! Bringing the power of his word and Spirit into this situation, he used Elijah to break the darkness and to draw people back to himself. This fascinating encounter with Elijah draws out his significance in God's plan and provides us with practical help to live for Christ in the spiritual darkness of the twenty-first century. Each chapter includes questions and points for reflection, making this an ideal book to be used in small groups or for personal study and devotion.

Simon Robinson is the senior minister of Walton Evangelical Church, Chesterfield, England. He has also written several other books, all published by Day One, including *Jesus, the life-changer, Improving your quiet time, Opening up 1 Timothy*, and *God, the Bible and terrorism*. He also preaches and teaches in Asia and the United States. He and his wife, Hazel, have two sons and one grandson.

Face2face with David, Vol. 1—Encountering Elijah the man after God's heart

MICHAEL BENTLEY

96PP, PAPERBACK

ISBN 978-1-84625-040-8

Raised in obscurity, young David would not have featured on a list of candidates for the future king of Israel—but God had different ideas! Read, here, about how God's magnificent plan unfolded in the life of this remarkable man and in the lives of those around him.

Michael Bentley worked as a bookshop manager and served in the British army before his call to the ministry. He has a diverse background, which includes freelance religious reporting for national and local radio and television, being a Religious Education teacher, and holding pastorates in Surrey, South East London, and Berkshire. He is also closely involved with his local community as a member of various committees and councils. Now retired, he still preaches regularly and has a ministry of writing, with some ten books in print and more in preparation. He lives in Bracknell with his wife, Jenny, and has five children and six grandchildren.

Michael Bentley has an enviable knowledge of the Bible and an admirably simple way of relating its events, and then interweaving the stories with their relevance to our life. Thus, we see how the actions related in the Bible can still be appropriate today in the way we live our lives.

PEOPLE IN THE PASSION OF JESUS

Opening up Psalms

ROGER ELLSWORTH

224PP, PAPERBACK

ISBN 978–1–84625–005–7

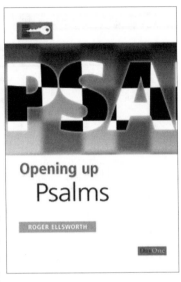

The Psalms, the longest book in the Bible, has been described as the national hymn-book of the people of Israel in the Old Testament. Full of emotion, expressing the believer's response to various experiences, and full of theology, these psalms give wonderful counsel to us today, both in our day-to-day life and in our worship. Roger Ellsworth competently leads us through the different kinds of psalms, first giving the 'big picture', then 'zooming in' to look at the detail of some of the psalms in closer perspective.

Roger Ellsworth has served as pastor of Immanuel Baptist Church, Benton, Illinois, since 1988. He and his wife, Sylvia, have two adult sons and one grandson. He is the author of eighteen books. He has also served as president of the Illinois Baptist State Association and as chairman of the Board of Trustees of South Eastern Baptist Theological Seminary. He is the author of some thirty books, including *What the Bible Teaches about Angels; Moses: God's Man for Challenging Times; The God of All Comfort; Face2Face with Samuel* and *Opening up Philippians*.

PEOPLE IN THE PASSION OF JESUS

Opening up Luke's Gospel

GAVIN CHILDRESS

224PP, PAPERBACK

ISBN 978–1–84625–030–9

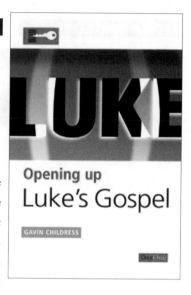

Opening up
Luke's Gospel
GAVIN CHILDRESS

Day One

The Gospel of Luke makes remarkable reading. It introduces us to many people the other Gospels don't mention; it shows the compassion of Jesus in a special way; it is the only Gospel written by a Gentile. Let Gavin Childress guide you through its message in easy stages, and there is plenty to think (and talk) about in the discussion points at the end of each chapter.

Gavin Childress and his wife Kathy have six children (three girls and three boys). Gavin pursued a career in social work until he was called to the ministry. He has been pastor of Grace Baptist Chapel in Tottenham, London, since 1987. He would love to see every Christian thoroughly enthusiastic about the study and application of the Gospels. Gavin is co-author with Audrey Dooley of *Reading your Bible—A starter's guide*, also published by Day One.

There is no better way for the newcomer to learn of Jesus Christ than to read through one of them as it introduces the God-man, not in abstract theories but in the encounters and conversations of everyday life. Gavin Childress has written a clear guide to Luke's Gospel that is well-suited to assist the first-time reader through what may be strange territory, explaining its setting in history and in the whole Bible, and-even more-bringing Jesus near to the issues and concerns of today.

John Nicholls, London City Mission

PEOPLE IN THE PASSION OF JESUS

Opening up Psalms

PHILIP H HACKING

96PP, PAPERBACK

ISBN 978–1–84625–042–2

Opening up
Hebrews

PHILIP HACKING

The letter to the Hebrews is a challenging document for our multi-faith age with its stress on the uniqueness of Jesus Christ in his person and work. In its call to come to Jesus 'outside the camp' it reminds us of the need for sacrifice in the Christian church. Yet it is full of the assurance of hope in Christ.

In its context and in its relevance for today Hebrews brings a special word to all who are in danger of losing heart or choosing the easy way in life. This book comes with a spiritual health warning!

Philip Hacking is a retired Anglican minister, vicar of Christ Church Fulwood, Sheffield, for almost thirty years and rector of St Thomas's Edinburgh for the previous ten years. He is former chairman of the Keswick Convention, of Word Alive (Spring Harvest) and of Reform (action group within the Church of England). He is married to Margaret with two children and five grandchildren. In retirement, he has a wide itinerant preaching ministry and is an occasional author.

Philip Hacking … lengthy pastoral experience is invaluable in capturing and communicating this important aspect of a much-neglected book and therefore makes it accessible to those who are keen to understand but daunted by the obvious difficulties in getting to grips with the text.

MICHAEL PLANT, GENERAL SECRETARY OF EFCC

PEOPLE IN THE PASSION OF JESUS

PEOPLE IN THE PASSION OF JESUS